Muscle
CARS

Muscle

CARS

RICHARD NICHOLS

Exeter Books

NEW YORK

A Bison Book

CONTENTS

INTRODUCTION

AMERICAN CARS ARE BIG. There's no other way of looking at it, and calling them compacts or sub-compacts just doesn't make a bit of difference: American cars are big. The concept of the small car is relatively new to the auto industry in Detroit - it wasn't until the early '50s that any major manufacturer went into series production with a two-seater, and although there were several attempts by other makers to cash in on a new market only Corvette had the staying power to sell alongside the nimble European imports. With a design and race heritage earned on tight racetracks from the beginning of the century, the small sportscars could run rings around the big sedans from Motor City. This ability, coupled with an expertise for producing large power outputs from small high-revving engines was completely at odds with the big and lazy powerplants which propelled Detroit's products.

Although Ford and General Motors were continually locked in a grim sales battle the impetus between them was to sell more cars rather than make better ones. Although GM could have built better cars than Ford, or vice versa, neither did – because they didn't have to. They just made them the same and marketed them hard. Practically all the advances being made during the '50s were of a cosmetic nature. Ford were still relying on their flathead V8, introduced by Henry in 1932 with the Model B. Although GM produced the fabled smallblock V8 in 1955 - their first V8 since the '20s – they resisted the arrival of the disk brake for years, refusing to spend money on the tooling. Fuel injection had been around for ages, had been in massive production during the war, mostly on aircraft engines, yet it was almost 15 years after 1945 before it appeared on a GM engine. Chassis design and development was not astoundingly advanced, suspension remained likewise stagnant.

Clearly something had to be done, but any kind of progress in the auto industry is necessarily ponderous, and it can take years to translate racetrack success into production-line advances. Instead of attempting to compete with the imports on level terms Detroit offered the younger, performance-oriented element among its

This is one of the few situations in which the musclecar still survives – and excels. As always, brute power is well-suited to drag racing's ¼-mile dash.

customers an alternative, based on homegrown motorsport. Following the hotrodders' ethos of slapping vast engines into small cars to produce phenomenal straight line performance for the drag strip, Detroit sought a way to offer the racers the same performance direct from the factory, and in the early '60s it was Pontiac who found the answer and set all the trends which would last for the next ten years.

April 1963 saw the White House/Kremlin hotline installed. Only a few months later John F Kennedy made his *Ich bin ein Berliner* speech at the Berlin Wall shortly before the signing of the nuclear test ban treaty by American, Russia and Great Britain. Adding to the swelling sense of purpose and destiny which was so much a hallmark of the early '60s Martin Luther King told America 'I have a dream' that August and Kennedy presented the Civil Rights Bill to Congress although neither he, nor Nobel Peace Prize-winner Martin Luther King would live to see its ambitions properly realised.

In a music scene populated by The Four Seasons, Paul and Paula, The Chiffons and 'Little' Stevie Wonder, America's biggest-selling single, lasting five weeks at the top, was *Sugar Shack*, by Jimmy Gilmer and the Fireballs.

Booker T's *Green Onions* (later to become the street racing theme from *American Graffiti*) had been released in 1962; at about the same time that the Beach Boys released *Surfin Safari*, which they followed up with *Surfin USA* in 1963, giving California an apparent monopoly on sun, sea, sand, surf and pretty blondes.

In 1963 Brian Wilson's interest in hotrodding and drag racing - which had both been exclusively Californian properties for some while – surfaced, together with the Beach Boys' long association with the newly-emergent Jan and Dean. The two bands between them produced a series of songs related to the Californian lifestyle. *Little Deuce Coupe, Fun Fun Fun, Little Old Lady from Pasadena* and *409* were mixed in with an assortment of surfing music to create an image of the West Coast which, while it may not have been strictly accurate, was blessed with longevity and still persists. The Beach Boys and Jan and Dean threw their respective record companies into hysterics because they kept appearing on each other's singles and albums – Brian Wilson reputedly sang lead on Jan and Dean's hit *Dead Man's Curve* – a prophetic song about a race between a Corvette and a Jaguar XKE which saw both cars off the road. In 1966, on a LA street second only to the

7

The outward signs of muscle were vitally important: the badgework, the shaker hoods, the open chromed carb throats, they all had a message to deliver.

legendary Van Nuys for cruising and street racing, Jan Berry was seriously injured, in fact all but killed, when he wrecked his Corvette on Whittier Blvd in a smash which left him paralyzed for a year and effectively ended the duo's singing career.

It wasn't until the '70s, when the era was over and shrouded in the warm afterglow of nostalgia that the real hotrodders musician appeared, and in an atmosphere pervaded by movies like *American Graffiti, Vanishing Point, Bullitt, White Line Fever, Two-lane Blacktop, The Getaway* and even *Dirty Mary and Crazy Larry* (all out of *Easy Rider* by *The Wild One*) came Bruce Springsteen, kicking off with *Born to Run* in 1975 and following it up three years later with *Racing in the Street*.

Nothing less than an ode to the period and the racers themselves, the song captured and encapsulated a time when every license-holder in America under the age of 25 had sneakers, blue jeans, a pack of cigarettes rolled into the sleeve of his T-shirt and a street-legal race car in his backyard. 'Got a '69 Chevy with a 396, fuelie heads and a Hurst on the floor', went the song, dedicated in lyric, heart and soul to 'all the shut down strangers and hot rod angels rumbling through this Promised land'.

Sheikh Yamani and Ralph Nader between them made certain that this era, populated by the vast firebreathing monsters which came to be known as the musclecars, was shortlived and will never come again, and it vanished in the mists of a new period of automotive austerity, personified by odd/even rationing and riots at the pumps. But although the time has gone the cars still remain as monuments to a bygone day, because hardware that tough doesn't disappear too easily, despite the horrific rate of attrition which the streetcars of the time managed to maintain. Every so often you'll meet one on the street, and you don't have to see it to know it's coming, because there's no sound on earth like the howl of a big-inch V8 mixed with the scream of spinning rubber which announces the arrival of the baddest streetfighter in town . . .

If you've got it . . . make sure everybody knows about it. Badgework, emblems and signwriting played an important role in identifying the fully-loaded streetracer from the family sedan.

PONTIAC GTO

To many the word musclecar means nothing at all; to others it means one thing and one thing only – the Pontiac GTO. There is no doubt at all that the GTO was the first, original musclecar, produced before the word had been coined, legendary before phrase caught up with fable.

The horsepower race had really got into its stride with the advent of Chrysler's 331 hemi in 1951. The hemi – hemispherical cylinder head – provides a number of advantages over other kinds of head simply by increased volumetric and thermal efficiency which translate on to the road as raw power. With only minor modifications the hemi was good for around 350hp and properly modified gave drag racers 1000hp. With Hillborn injection it appeared at Indianapolis in 1953, giving 400hp, and stock hemi engines in the Chrysler 300 dominated the 1955 and '56 NASCAR circuits. No doubt the story would have gone on longer but in 1957 the AMA agreed to de-emphasize'

racing, all of their members gradually withdrawing from competition.

Also hit by the decision to back out of racing were GM's Pontiac division. With sliding sales and eventual closure its only future, Pontiac had been placed in the hands of Semon 'Bunkie' Knudsen in 1956. His mission to rescue the company with market research, then a relatively in-exact science, which revealed that Pontiac, who had been building sedate straight eight sedans since dot, had no discernible image in the marketplace at all. Knudsen saw this as an advantage, since it allowed him to select and project whatever image he chose.

Following on the heels of this incredible piece of optimism came one of the most farsighted marketing decisions ever made. Knudsen saw and recognized the results of the postwar baby boom, saw the sheer numbers of the rapidly growing youth market and went straight for it. Not only did Pontiac have no image in the marketplace, but these youngsters (many of whom were not old enough to hold a

Left: The last of the steel-fronted 'Goats' were made in 1967; when they were replaced in 68 by the Endura nosecones the quad headlamps were also phased out and replaced by concealed lamps (**below**).

Others have caught on.
But they haven't caught up.

Imagine, for a moment, that you are in charge of designing an answer to the GTO. And that this has been your task since The Great One first rumbled into reality, sending shock waves through your offices.

Each year you've sent your answer into the streets. And, each year, seen it change into something merely medi-ocre alongside GTO's Hurst shifter, bulging hood scoops and Wide-Track. And, this year, humiliated by an in-credible new kind of bumper.

And just when you're getting the hang of its extra-cost Ram Air (yours will surely out-GTO GTO next year),

you find Pontiac has improved theirs. With a new high-lift cam, larger swirled exhaust valves, new freer breathing combustion chambers.

When the Car of the Year is improved even before the year is over, can your car ever catch up? Pontiac Motor Division

The Great One by Pontiac

Anxious for 5 color pictures, specs and decals of the Great Wide-Tracks? Don't be. Send 30¢ (50¢ outside U.S.A.) to: '68 Wide-Tracks, P.O. Box 888E, 196 Wide-Track Blvd , Pontiac, Michigan 49056

Above: Naturally the 1968 advertising shots majored on the new front end, and the copy gently reminded the reader that the GTO was the one which started the whole thing off.

driving license) had no image of the market, providing a huge blank sheet on which Pontiac could imprint any image they chose, all without offending any existing brand loyalty.

Using the new-in-1955 V8 engine, Knudsen and his team went all-out for performance, producing 130mph stormers with 300hp under the hood. Pontiac entered NASCAR racing and won at Daytona in 1957, 1958 and again in 1959, tacitly ignoring the AMA 'ban' on motor-sport. Pontiac, using the new 'Super Duty' version of the V8, were practically unbeatable on the dragstrip, backed up their sport involvement with a bewildering catalog of performance parts available from the factory, created per-formance packages which could be fitted through the dealership program without affecting warranty and rose from number six to number three in the new car sales league.

Then in 1963 GM decided to adopt the AMA resolution and issued their infamous 'no racing' edict, giving the entire company orders to ship out all performance parts within 14 days, just like that. Quite why GM waited six years to comply with the resolution and then do so at such incredibly short notice is not clear, although many unkind souls will point out that their ban was almost coincidental

Left: By 1970 the era was drawing to a close. Instead of more power, the Judge and its stablemates got more decals.
Above: Still wearing its plastic nosecone, the straight 1970 GTO had regained its familiar 'face' and the quad lamps were out front again.

with the arrival of the Ford 427 ohv engine and Ford's announcement of a multi-milion dollar investment in a racing program which would include the Total Perform- ance ethos, the Mustang and the legendary Carroll Shelby.

Whatever the reason, it left Pontiac high and dry with nothing to back up previous success, and cars cannot be sold on the basis of nostalgia. Unable to get near a race track, not allowed to use race success in advertising, Pontiac had to find a new angle. Advertising man Jim Wangers and the magnetic John Z DeLorean went to Pon- tiac chief engineer Peter Estes with a plan to put the big 389 V8 into the Tempest, a four-cylinder compact which was just about the smallest vehicle in the range. This was basically only the hotrodders' technique which had been around since the late '30s; and which had gradually grown

into legitimate drag racing, the fastest-growing form of motorsport in the USA, but it had never been attempted by a manufacturer before.

In any case it set the entire trend for the musclecar of the future, since the GTO was not a new car in any sense of the word; it was simply a selection of options available on the Tempest, and was accordingly launched as the Tempest GTO. Later GTO packages were available on the LeMans and Catalina, but the GTO was never a car in its own right. Neither was it the only musclecar which had no existence outside the option boxes on a dealer order form. The 389 engine itself, which formed the basis of the GTO package, was option three hundred and twenty-something, and some buyers didn't even see it at the bottom of the form. It was this lack of ground-up design for what was potentially such a powerful car which would be the root of much criticism later on for the breed in general, not just the GTO.

But that would be much later on, when the GTO had developed its mystique. At first it was a car to be kept

Above: Even with the 'cleaner' front end the Endura allowed, the message was still there loud and clear. The GTO legend stands out on the grille.

hidden at the back of workshops and tended to late nights or weekends. The development program was carried out virtually in secret, because although the new car was officially designated a sportscar there was little doubt that its real business was racing, albeit in private rather than company hands. Estes did not even tell Pontiac what was going on. The no-racing rule meant that Pontiac's small cars could not be fitted with any engine over 330ci without breaking company rules. The GTO was eventually shown to the board as a 326, with the big 389 as an option, but even then the reaction was violently antagonistic, and DeLorean later said that the meeting came close to degenerating into a fistfight as Board members assured him that the car would never sell

Eventually compromise was reached, largely because word of the new car had leaked out and dealers were already beginning to send in orders, and the Board decided to go for a limited build of 5000 units. In that first year the GTO sold 32,000 units, making it the most successful first-year model Pontiac had ever introduced. Wangers believed that they could have sold twice that number if the cars had been available, and the point was proved that next year when they did exactly that.

What they were selling was a car which set the tone of the next ten years as far as US performance motoring was concerned. Basically it was a five-seat sedan with a huge engine, giving it sportscar performance, at least in the forward direction. Externally it had dummy hood scoops

and bore the legend GTO on the radiator, front fenders, rear quarters, trunk lid and dash panel as a triangular red, white and blue crest. Slight changes to the suspension, making it stiffer and more suitable to the kind of power the engine could deliver, were made, and that was it; the stuff of which dreams and legends are made.

Like its later imitators the GTO built its success on the incredibly long list of options which made it possible for any buyer to order a car tailor-made to his or her personal specifications, from center console through Hurst floor-shift right up to the three-carburetor Tri-Power manifold pack. This was set up to run only the center carburetor for most conditions, right up to speeds of around 100mph. It was then that the two outer throats opened; then or when hard acceleration was called for, and with the pedal down to the floor 12 square inches of bore opened in the top of the manifold and began dragging air and fuel into the engine. The GTO had a 'noticeable' power surge around 3300rpm as it rocketed to its rated output of 348bhp.

Large numbers of purists took exception to Pontiac's use of the GTO designation (Gran Turismo Omologato), which was drawn straight from sportscar racing, and almost alone Car and Driver magazine spoke out on Pontiac's behalf, claiming that the Motown GTO was every bit as good as Ferrari GTO, already something of a legend. Car and Driver took so much stick after this that they set out to prove the point, and arranged a test between the two cars. On the day their GTO had only seven cylinders working

thanks to a dud piston, so they brought a giant 421ci Catalina (not much smaller than the flying boat) into play. At the end of the day they said that the Catalina could outdrag the Ferrari with ease but was less agile and thus lost out on the circuit. Given some stiffer suspension, such as might be fitted for NASCAR racing they concluded that Modena could beat it on a circuit only if they fielded a prototype racing car. Furthermore the Ferrari GTO cost $14,000, the Pontiac GTO $4000. Loaded with every possible option including power brakes, metal brake linings, the handling package, you name it, the GTO was still $10,000 cheaper than the Ferrari and could do everything the illustrious Italian was capable of and sometimes more.

Almost accidentally Pontiac had given America a brand new toy to play with, a five or six seat sedan which left the line like a Phantom out of a catapult. '0-100 in 11.8 seconds' said the front cover of Car and Driver in March of '64. Although the GTO had set a whole new set of technical standards – it was the first to have the Hurst shifter available as a factory-fitted option – it also set the trends for the way the rest of the musclecar breed was presented, marketed and hyped. The GTO was on the back of cornflake packets, was given away in competitions and was in stores everywhere as a model kit by Monogram.

Below: By 1971 front end styling had become leaner, more aggressive. But it still retained the 'nostrils' and the familiar Pontiac look.

FORD

In early 1963 Ford, like everybody else, had big-inch engines on offer, and like everybody else they sold them in big sedans like the 'intermediate-size' Fairlane and Falcon. Their sales message was that the big 425hp V8 carried the huge cars up hills 'like a homesick Swiss yodeller'. Although the ads go on to mention the massive horsepower available – and even include mention of the Total Performance Program, but in tiny lettering tucked into a corner – the image was hardly one of rip-roaring streetracers burning up the quarter-mile. It was more the family man who likes enough power under the hood to be sure of getting the wife and kids away into the countryside for a weekend without a lot of huffing and puffing.

This was a time, remember, when the market still was the family man. Valentina Tereshkova had just become the first woman in space and NASA was still into the Mercury Program (in this year Major Gordon Cooper orbited the earth 22 times on a Mercury mission); Rachel Carson wrote the morbidly prophetic 'Silent Spring', and in Britain four young guys from Liverpool were creating a sensation with their strange singing, screaming fans and 'long' hair which actually touched the collar at the back and partly covered their ears!

The young drivers on the streets either borrowed the family car or they drove an old scrapper, although the adventurous ones were slipping fast V8s into old cars from the '30s and '40s. Straight off the lake beds the SCTA graduated to proper dragstrips at places like Santa Barbara, running the old cars with Ford's flathead V8 and the Chrysler 300, making 'proper' drag racing a reality and, along the way, a subject for factory interest. Indeed the factories became so wrapped up in drag racing that they began using their successes on the strip in advertising, and there was eventually a class of racing designated FX – factory experimental – which eventually metamorphosed into the class now known as Funny Car, finally via the medium of Dyno Don Nicholson's fiberglass Mercury Comet Cyclone from 1966. Unofficially there was an awful lot of factory participation in off-track events, and there were a number of vehicles seen late at night on Detroit's Woodward Avenue which were nothing less than factory try-outs and which later appeared as race cars or even production vehicles.

Ford's Total Performance Project was launched by Lee Iacocca, who wanted to get Ford away from building these straightforward 'people-haulers' and in the process worked his way from a small sales job through to President of the Ford Motor Company. In April 1963 he made a speech to the Press which was the starting point of the Total Performance Program. Speaking of factory involvement in motor racing – any motor racing – Iacocca said that the Ford attitude was based on the belief that racing improves the breed, that anybody entering a race event using a Ford car or Ford power deserved factory support and that Ford intended to use race success as part of its advertising campaigns, hence the 'race on Sunday, sell on Monday' slogan. Finally, Iacocca summed up: 'Our philosophy', he said, 'is based on TOTAL PERFORMANCE.'

This was an attitude which Ford had long held but had so far kept reasonably quiet about, as those early ads show. But from now on the game was changing. Ford had been involved in motorsport for a long times. When the hotrodders were forced off the Muroc lakebed so that it could, as Edwards AFB, be home to Chuck Yeager and loads of the Right Stuff, they had been using the old flathead V8 in abundance. Then in 1960 Ford introduced their 352 High-Performance engine which would be the basis of the Super/Stock class. Many factories had put out high-performance engines, with high-compression pistons, hot cam, dual carburetors and dual exhausts, but Ford expanded even more effort, strengthening the bottom end of the engine so that it could give its best without coming apart at the seams. This engine was the basis of the later hot engines like the 406 and the 427, and was the formula which the other manufacturers set out to follow.

In 1961 Ford dealers became even more involved with the developing performance program, with the introduction of the 6bbl tri-power package which, bolted on top of the 390 V8, lifted output from 375 to a respectable 400hp.

Right: Two faces of Ford advertising from the sixties. Selling the same thing to different people, only one of them mentions Total Performance.
Below: The luxury end of the ponycar market, the big-block Torino from 68 shows its heritage in every line.

Over the past eight years
Myrtle Tower's hair has been

swirled   whirled   uncurled

But her cars have been Ford, Ford, Ford.
It's a trend. Ford owners are buying
Fords again in record-breaking numbers.
Why? Because their Fords gave them
a lot of mileage without a lot of
headaches. Myrtle's '67 is the best yet—
the strongest, quietest Ford ever built.
And it offers all sorts of new ideas—like a
SelectShift transmission you can use auto-
matically or manually. Ride Ford's New
Wave for '67. It could
start a long friendship.

STRONG CARS MAKE STRONG FRIENDS

| New ideas available from Ford for '67: ☐ All Ford automatic transmissions are now SelectShift, can be used automatically or manually, according to the driving situation. ☐ Front power disc brakes available on all models. | ☐ Convenience control panel has lights to warn when fuel's low, door's ajar. One switch locks all doors. ☐ Stereo Tape/Radio system comes as an integrated unit, smartly styled into instrument panel. ☐ Magic Doorgate for | wagons (standard) swings out like a door for people, down like a tailgate for cargo. ☐ Ford Motor Company Lifeguard-Design safety features are standard on all 1967 Fords. | YOU'RE AHEAD IN A FORD **FORD** |

1966 Fairlane GT

The great thing about Fairlane's new GT/A automatic is it can stop being automatic.

Comes a time in the life of every manual shift when you wish you had an automatic transmission. Comes also a time in the life of every automatic transmission when you wish you had a manual shift.

What a perfect time to spring the new Fairlane GT/A Sportshift.

This Fairlane option gives you the option of automatic convenience or manual fun. It also gives you a 335-horsepower V-8, which lifts it out of the Amusing Gadget class fast.

Under the GT/A's console mounted T-handle selector is a quadrant reading "P-R-N-D-2-1." Through the P-R-N-D part it's pure automatic.

Makes all the shifting decisions for you. But flick into 1 or 2 and it's your move. You decide how long to hold it and when to shift. Here in

one fell swoop is manual gearbox flexibility with the ease of automatic drive only a shift away.

What you can accomplish with a 390-cubic-inch hydraulic lifter V-8 harnessed to this GT/A setup—and packed into Fairlane's trim dimensions—is something you'll have to work out with your imagination.

Progress, it's wonderful. Sportshift, it's unbelievable—until you try it.

AMERICA'S
TOTAL PERFORMANCE CARS
FORD
MUSTANG · FALCON · FAIRLANE
FORD · THUNDERBIRD

These engines also carried Magnafluxed pistons and rods, solid lifter cams and special valvetrains from the factory, but the tri-power package was dealer-installed for the first year on Starliners and Sunliners. A year later, having proved itself in NHRA events, it became a factory option. As such it meant that cars fitted with the package were eligible for Stock class drag races, where the previous year's dealer-fitted packages had been forced to run in Super/Stock. By the same token the Galaxie fastbacks prepared by Holman and Moody by grafting Starliner roof sections onto the big convertible were made acceptable for NASCAR racing by listing the alteration as a conversion kit in the catalog.

Run at Bonneville in 1962, car No. 28 which was supposedly 'sponsored' by a North Carolina dealership but which was really one of these specials bored out by Ford to 483ci, set 46 National and International records. The trick of making performance parts options on stock sedans to enable them to run in lower classes at race events was one which was developed and refined and which characterized the entire musclecar period and defined the formula which other manufacturers set out to follow.

Maintaining the Ford involvement in motorsport, the 427 appeared in 1963 fitted to the big fastback Galaxies which barnstormed their way through the NASCAR series that year, and even in an F-100 XL pickup which ran consistent high 12s at over 100mph throughout the season. An all-aluminum version of the Fairlane engine powered Jim Clark's Lotus at Indy, and a Falcon Sprint came first in its class in the Monte Carlo Rally. At practically every level and in every type of performance competition there were drivers and teams 'sponsored' by a local Ford dealership. All had factory support, some were merely campaigning the latest factory products which provided Ford with all the kudos of a good win and were deniable as local dealer efforts if they lost badly. Holman and Moody did much work for and with Ford, and people like Bob Tasca, with a Ford dealership at Providence, RI, always had a plentiful supply of lightweight fiberglass Galaxies for sale and campaigned a rare factory lightweight known as the Robert F Tasca Special in A/FX.

Above: By 1970 the Torino Cobra had grown more angles and borrowed black paint and a famous name to keep its image high.
Below: The way we were. An advertising shot of the most successful car of the decade – a Mustang fastback.

MUSTANG

Meanwhile, back at the ranch, Lee Iacocca (who had been in front-line sales when Ford had converted their two-seat Thunderbird into a four-seat limousine) could still remember the number of people who had pleaded with the firm to bring back the two-seater. In response to that he began to look at a replacement for the two-seat T-bird, and a first prototype was prepared. Its initial parameters were almost identical to those laid down for Corvette ten years earlier; small, peppy and inexpensive. The prototype was a mid-engined wedge on a 90-inch wheelbase with the V4 motor from the Cardinal and was an extremely pretty little car. Iacocca rejected it almost immediately on the grounds that it could never become a volume production car; Mustang was scheduled to reach 100,000 units in the first year. Although Mustang 2 retained many of the styling characteristics of the first car it was, unlike its ill-fated predecessor, immediately recognizable as a Mustang to modern eyes.

The eventual production prototype appeared on a conventional 108-inch chassis, had four seats and was powered by a 170ci Falcon straight six or the small 260 V8. It was the greatest single automotive success story of the '60s, selling 680,000 units in the first nine months of production and setting an all-time record for first-year sales of a new model. It was introduced in April and by September the power units had become either the 200 six or the bored-out 289, but this was just the start of the progression to big horsepower.

Traditionally for a musclecar, the Mustang appeal was hidden in the option boxes on the dealer order forms. Aside from being able to order a basic compact for marketing customers could choose a full-house race car via the possible mix of three or four-speed stick-shifts, handling package, disk brakes, power steering, airconditioning, tachometer, bench or bucket seats, you name it. And naturally there was a selection of special badgework, stripes and body moldings all available on option. There was also a choice of body styles, all based on the long hood and short deck which were the work of David Ash, Joe Oros and Gayle Halderman at Ford's design studios and which characterized the Mustang and its later imitators (and for which they were christened Ponycars in its honor). It came as a hardtop, a convertible or a fastback coupe, styles which would stay with it virtually unchanged for years. Although convertibles sold well initially (100,000 in 1965) figures fell progressively and in 1970 only 7000 were sold. The fastback did well, at 77,000 in 1965, but the big success was the notchback: 500,000 units in the first year.

The first big facelift came in 1969, providing a taste of what was in store as Mustang became longer, lower and wider, growing dummy hood scoops and vents and a rear deck spoiler, and added the 351 Mach 1 to the lineup. That wasn't the first engine change, and there had already been some substantial alterations and additions under the hood.

Left: As the years went by the Mustang grew in size and became heavier in appearance. Compare the Boss 302 with the 65 convertible (**above and below**). This was its introductory year and shows its classic lines.

Above: Even with the altered styling the Mustangs from 68 onwards still looked pretty tough.
Below: This is how they're remembered best.

1967 saw the arrival of the 320hp 390ci motor and the following year witnessed the introduction of the 427, which knocked out 335hp.

All car manufacturers announce their new models in the preceding fall, so that the 1985 cars are launched in late '84. In keeping with this Ford had dubbed the next decade the 'sizzlin' seventies' even before they started, but how were they to know that the sizzle they expected would be the sound of the big-horse engines fizzling out. The Boss Mustangs entered the new decade as the spearhead of Ford's muscle program, alongside the Mach 1. Between them there were six body styles and seven engine options available, from the 200-inch, 115hp straight six all the way up to the new top-of-the-range Boss 429, which carried Ford's NASCAR hemi engine onto the street, delivering 375bhp.

But there was little more than a year left, and in late 1970 Ford abandoned most of its Trans-Am, USAC and NASCAR events, and began to tone down the Mustang to face the austerity to come, producing tame and weakened cars, allocating to the original ponycar the same fate of emasculation suffered by its predecessor, the Thunderbird.

SHELBY AMERICAN

Forced by a heart condition to retire from racing – in which he had been a successful enough driver – Texan Carroll Shelby maintained his interest in the sport by turning to the manufacture of race cars. He had raced on circuits right across the USA and Europe, driven for Porsche, won the 1959 Le Mans 24 Hours for Aston Martin and was familiar with many of the obscure cars which populated the European racetracks of the '50s. He was also familiar with the way they out-handled practically anything built in the USA, although they couldn't match the big V8s for brute power. His was the idea to combine the best of both worlds, matching nimble European chassis and suspension to an American V8. The body and chassis unit he chose was from the tiny AC company at Thames Ditton, England, and the body was an open two-seater with a very long hood and a tiny cramped cockpit with zero luxury, perched in front of a short, bobbed deck.

Shelby's choice of engine went to Ford; his proposition arrived at a time when the company was looking to produce a sportscar anyway – they were already at work on the Mustang. And Shelby himself, although a racing driver, was quite well aware that building race cars was not an economically viable idea, so his car was designed to be a street car as well. The prototype, built in a California workshop which Shelby shared with Dean Moon, used the new 221 smallblock V8 and was destined for magazine loan

long before it was finished. It went out in bright aluminum for the first test and was painted bright yellow for the second, in which guise it made the cover of *Road and Track*. Subsequently it was repainted each time it went out, so that each magazine thought they'd got a different car, and it seemed that the Cobra was in mass production.

That was something destined to be part of the Cobra story; each and every car was hand-built and as improvements to design were discovered so they were built into the line, so there are virtually no two cars the same. Furthermore, as the improvements became known many Cobra owners brought theirs back to have them modified. So it was that although the first 75 Cobras had the 221 engine fitted, bored out to 260, when Ford offered the engine as a 289 it was immediately used for the Cobra from then on, and many of the existing owners brought their 260 back for a transplant.

It wasn't until 1962 that Shelby tried the car out on a racetrack officially, and at Riverside in October that year a red Cobra driven by Billy Krause built up a lead of a mile and a half over the rest of the field before breaking a stub axle. It was a silly retirement but that didn't matter: the potential of the car had been clearly established and for the next three years it would dominate virtually every kind of motor race.

In 1965 the Cobras brought the USA the ultimate accolade and its first (and only) World Manufacturer's Championship, finally realizing Shelby's stated ambition to 'blow Ferrari's ass off'. To win, the FIA Cobras had done just that at Daytona, Sebring, Oulton Park, Nurburgring, Rossfield, Rheims and, rubbing salt in the wound, Monza. The only real disappointment had come at Le Mans when the Cobras ran in second behind the red Ferraris, but even in that defeat were the seeds of a future victory; running alongside the Cobras in the '65 season were their stablemates, the infant Ford GTs, just cutting their teeth on the international

Below: A legend after four years in production, the peerless Shelby Cobra, this one built in 1966.

race circuit and not yet placed under the care of Shelby.

At the dragstrips of America the Cobra was virtually unstoppable and was eventually ruled out; privately owned Cobras were dishing out humble pie on oval racetracks in every State and in November of '65 Craig Breedlove took a Cobra to Bonneville; when the dust settled he had taken 23 National and International records.

Away from the raceways. the Shelby magic was also being applied to road cars. As long ago as '64 Ford were advertising 'Cobra Tonic', which was 'Dr Shelby's marvellous elixir for Fairlanes, Falcons and Galaxies, in ten strengths up to 343hp.' Then came the streetgoing Cobras, cars which have been a benchmark, a kind of automotive touchstone, ever since. Beyond any doubt the Cobra is the car to which all sportscars are ultimately compared, and although such comparisons are fairly meaningless, all have been found lacking.

In 1963 Ford introduced the 427 engine and, no surprise, it found its way under the Cobra hood and lent a whole new meaning to snakebite. Out of the 1011 Cobras built by Shelby 356 were the real screamers. The 427,

Main picture and above: Rarity and good looks made the Cobra a true classic. Blinding acceleration helps as well.
Top right: Even rarer still, and even faster one of the 356 Shelby-built 427 Cobras.

coil-sprung, alloy-bodied Cobras had a performance curve which was all but vertical. 485 incredible horsepower translated into 0-60 in 4.3 seconds (although some versions could do it in 3.8), 0-100 in 8.6, 0-100 and stop in 14 seconds, standing quarters in 12.2 seconds, and a top speed of 162mph. This was an Exocet for the road, except that in 1966 the armament factories hadn't got anything that fast.

The press were enthusiastic, if that's the right understatement: 'It's only fair to warn you that out of the 300 guys who switched to the 427 Cobra only two went back to women . . .', 'unless you own real estate near the Bonneville salt flats you'll never see the top end,' 'a Cobra is a race car with enough legality built into it so you can drive it on the street,' 'the only accessory which comes with the Cobra is a Highway Patrol Car in back of you. Way back . . .,' and perhaps most telling, 'I bought the 427 from Shelby on the spot and gave him a check, using my driver's licence for

identification. We both realized that it might be the last time either of us would see the document.'

In 1965, with the FIA Championship under his belt Shelby withdrew the Cobras from competition, and they were succeeded on the track by the Ford GT. Although the power had been by Ford, it was Shelby who'd won the championship, and Ford were anxious to secure their own trophies, and it was this 'mobile testbed', as they'd called it in 1964, which they were relying on. However there was little or no joy to be had from it until, in virtual desperation, the project was passed over to Shelby and the car immediately took Ferrari to the cleaners with a 1-2-3 procession of GT40s across the line in the 1966 Le Mans 24 hours.

At the same time as Shelby withdrew the Cobras from racing there appeared on the streets the latest hot Mustang: the Shelby GT350. Like the Cobra it was a car designed for racing. If it was driven on the street then it was

The tie-up between Shelby and the new Mustang was an obvious step for Ford to take in 1965. The GT350 was the first result.

not the kind of car to give big limo comforts; there were no compromises. Like the Cobra it was built on an individual basis and practically all of the 562 produced in 1965 were different. Modifications and improvements were added and if the line ran out of something then the cars were built without the part. The spec list for the GT350 shows what should have been there: 289 OHV Cobra engine with hi-riser aluminum manifold, four -barrel carburetor, tuned tubular exhaust with straight-through mufflers, extra capacity finned and baffled aluminum oil pan, Borg-Warner close-ratio four-speed gearbox in light alloy case, computer-designed competition suspension geometry with one-inch front roll bar, fully stabilized torque controlled rear axle with limited slip diff, Goodyear 130mph-rated performance Blue Dot tires, Kelsey-Hayes ventilated front disks with competition pads, wide drum rear brakes with metallic linings, Koni adjustable shock absorbers, lightweight fiberglass hood, instrument cluster with tachometer and oil pressure gauge, all black interior, quick ratio steering and a 350 identification sidestripe. And that was the street version. The competition version had an even higher specification, which included more fiberglass, bigger fuel tank and huge exhausts.

Above: Always strong on image, Ford's pinstriping and decal department excelled themselves with the Shelby Mustangs.

In this guise the cars were superb, but not profitable from the Ford point of view. Cost accountants from Dearborn made small, subtle changes to the production line after about 250 cars had been built, changes which Shelby was not happy about but which improved the appeal of the car. In fact it was improved so much that Hertz bought a large number to rent out; the GT350H was available to what Hertz thought were bored executives, all members of the Hertz Sports Car Club. And while Hertz management retained fond mental images of oil magnates gently reliving their youth on country backroads the GT350H was making guest appearances at every weekend drag meeting across

America. There are even stories of cars being returned on Monday mornings with spots under the carpets where a roll cage had been temporarily welded in.

The Mustang facelift in 1967 gave Shelby a small problem since it was now an altogether bigger car. It had become a luxury GT with airconditioning and other expensive options. In order to keep performance as the frontline option the Shelby cars had their own distinctive fiberglass front end to save a bit of weight, but the big news was under the hood. In 1967 the Shelby grew a new engine and the 428 GT500 became the car that everyone wanted to own. It was called the GT500 because Shelby thought it was a good name; reasoning which was as arbitrary as that which had christened the previous car on the basis that the distance from the engine shop to the assembly line was 'about' 350 feet.

With airconditioning, power steering, automatic gearbox and so on, the new cars were far more civilized and generally acceptable than the basic GT350 had been, which may be one reason why sales were far better. The other reason was probably linked with performance. Its advertised output was much lower than the 400hp it was capable of delivering; already there were problems with the antisocial musclecars and it was easier to sell and insure the 500 with a 'modified' performance spec. But what was written on paper didn't make a lot of odds; it was rumored that the GT500 could destroy a set of rear tires in a single evening of streetracing, and probably the rumor was

Below: The least popular but most common view of the GT 350.

enough to start most owners trying to find out if it was true.

These cars were the ones advertised as 'the Road Cars', and both Ford and Shelby were justifiably pleased with performance, handling and stopping – Total Performance up to the eyeballs, in fact. This countered much of the criticisms aimed at some of the other musclecars, especially the big sedan-based conversions like Chevelle, Catalina, even the Galaxies, which although they were phenomenally fast had little or no stopping ability, an exceptionally dangerous combination, as owners, insurance companies and junkyards were finding out.

But Ford were deeply committed to Total Performance as a sales tool, and in '67 Cobra production ended because Dearborn wanted to concentrate on the GT cars since they were a major boost to Mustang sales generally – sales which were gradually flagging, and had been slowly dropping almost since that first successful year. Shelby stayed with open-top cars, though, and in 1968 began production of some of the most desirable cars ever – the convertible GT350 and 500, a range which had the desired effect and began to boost sales.

In 1968 the GT350 dropped the 289 for the new 302, and in '69 the Mustang got another facelift which added more weight and forced Shelby to come up with something extra. Fiberglass was used for the front fenders as well as the hood, and cooling vents for the brakes were let into the sides. There were five ventilation inlets on the hood itself, and the GT350 was given the new 351 Windsor engine. Midway through the year Shelby introduced the 500KR (King of the Road), featuring the 428 Cobra Jet, engine, and it replaced the standard GT500 from then on.

The '60s, through which Shelby had done rather more than just survive, were drawing to a close, and there was a general awareness that things would never be the same again; there was probably no other period in history in which so much happened in such a compressed time-span. In '68 Martin Luther King was assassinated, Bobby Kennedy was shot in Los Angeles and Richard Nixon was elected President in a campaign which saw the 'Battle of Chicago' outside the Democrat convention which gave its nomination to the Humphrey/Muskie ticket.

The Beatles had gone from being pop giants into gurus of the hippie generation and begun to split; they played their last ever concert together in San Francisco the following year, as Neil Armstrong placed his feet on the surface of the Moon; he would never return, nor would the Beatles or the mood of their times.

Shelby were fighting battles on all fronts, not just street corners, and faced tough competition for their products from Ford's own Mustang streetfighters, the Boss 302, the Boss 429 and the Mach 1. Insurance was almost impossible to get on one of the Shelby cars – they had a horrific accident rate directly attributable to the fact that they had more power than most people knew what to do with – and they weren't alone. Some of the bigger vehicles from other factories – less powerful, perhaps, but without the suspension and braking refinements of the Shelbys - were also among the most crashed cars in the history of the auto industry. Word was out that there would soon be a Federal ban on horsepower advertising, plus an assortment of other regulations designed to obliterate the musclecars.

Shelby asked Ford President Lee Iacocca to release him from the Total Performance Program, and the remainder of the 1969 models were given airdams, black hood stripes and 1970 serial numbers, and these 601 cars were the last of the 14,368 Shelby Mustangs ever made.

PLYMOUTH

Ford declared war when the Mustang moved in on the Corvette in 1965, threatening once again the market which GM had virtually owned after Thunderbird had moved out for the more lucrative personal car four-seater sector in 1958. This time, though, it was not only going to be a battle of the two Detroit giants, because there were other makers interested in the fight.

Of necessity the motor industry is slow to react, slow to get things into production. Even minor modifications to an existing production car take time, and launching a brand new car is a process which traditionally takes years. Chevrolet had shown how fast they could move when they brought Corvette into admittedly limited and low-volume production only months after its rapturous acceptance at the 1953 New York Autorama. Now it was the turn of Plymouth to show their turn of speed and they did move more swiftly than anyone else, announcing the Barracuda only months after the launch of the Mustang.

Initially something of a stopgap, the first Barracudas were nothing more than heavily-disguised Valiants, given a fastback body style and, as Plymouth went to great pains to point out, the largest rear window glass ever fitted to an automobile — 14.4 square feet.

Plymouth had offered a performance option ever since the 1956 426 Fury, available either as a 365hp street car or in track versions at 415 and 425hp. But the first Barracudas, true to the musclecar breed, came only with the 100hp 170 slant six as standard; the 225ci 140hp six and the 180hp 273 V8 were options. Manual three-speed was standard, auto three-speed and the Hurst four-speed were options also. Incredibly, for what was designed to be the performance option, power brakes were just that: optional.

1965 saw only minor changes to the exterior, but big ones under the hood, mainly the Formula S package. This was not only designed to give the Barracuda more power but better handling as well. On top of the new 235hp Commando 273 V8, people checking the Formula S option

Below: Stablemate to the Dodge Challenger, the Road Runner package could be discreet; the rear wing wasn't always part of it.
Right; Plymouth's answer to the Mustang was the reworked Valiant, launched as the Barracuda.

1968

on the order blank got oversize front torsion bars, sway bar, high-rate springs and stiffer shocks. But while Barracuda was Plymouth's anti-Mustang weapon they were also forced to compete on other performance fronts with the likes of Pontiac and Dodge, and they went into the battle in late '63 with their 'orange monster.' Not a car, this was the 426-111 Super Stock hemi engine which was the power behind Plymouth's heavily advertised drag-racing 'vanishing act' which had produced 26 track records in one season and an 11.39 elapsed time. The advertising, carefully placed in all the performance magazines of the time, warned that the motor was built for competition only – in very small lettering, tucked away in a corner. Naturally it was only a year before they made the street hemi available, first off in the Belvedere, producing a five-seat sedan which delivered a whopping 425hp; just the thing in which middle-aged executives could nip round to the golf club.

Also part of the Belvedere lineup was the Satellite, and this was the real business end of Plymouth's performance attack so far. Available as a hardtop or convertible, it came only with a V8 engine; the 273 was standard, but there were four other options – 318, 383 or 426 wedge and the fabled 426 hemi. Straight off the showroom floor this was an AA/Stock drag race contender, and a ready-to-race NASCAR winner in which Richard Petty won the NASCAR Championship in 1967. The year also saw new additions to the Plymouth range and facelifts all round. Barracuda, Valiant and Fury were all-new for this model year and introduced in the Belvedere lineup were two models designated GTX. These were designed as straightforward high-performance cars and came with a 440 4-barrel V8 of some 375hp. Optional, and now reserved for the GTX alone, was the 426 street hemi, and to make the whole arrangement more the kind of thing you'd expect from a fast, high-performance missile of this nature it was given a heavy duty suspension setup, dual hood scoops, chrome dual exhaust outlets, 'pit stop' gas cap and optional stripes for the hood and rear deck. Front disk brakes were described in the advertising as 'popular options.'

To be fair though, the serious racer could, by sensible allocation of a few dollars and ticks in the right option boxes, produce a car from the showroom which was already up to track specification, and many did. What many others did was to choose a street car from the same order blank, ticking only those boxes which supplied forward power, neglecting those which concerned handling and stopping characteristics. This was true not only of Plymouths, but of all the cars competing in the musclecar bracket, and you only have to read the road tests of the time to find out. Many magazines, who went to the trouble of ordering their test cars with all the handling and braking packages which were available, still found them lacking in this department. European road testers, particularly, were horrified by what appeared to them as a complete lack of any handling capability beyond that normally found in a bouncing ball, and criticized accordingly. Even US magazine testers found the entire breed 'long on go, short on whoa,' and these were the top-handling models. Exactly what those cars with performance engines and no attention to the ride and handling can have been like to drive does not bear thinking about.

Except by insurance companies, who were by now beginning to think about it fairly seriously. The moment when auto manufacturers – all auto makers, not just one or two – would have to tell lies about power ratings was coming, but before then the insurers had worse to face than they had seen already. Meanwhile Barracuda was doing very well for itself. Although you could buy the 273 Commando V8 without adding any kind of handling option as well, Plymouth absolutely insisted that front disks were mandatory on the 383, but even then *Car and Driver* found the brakes lacking when they lined the Barracuda up in a six-car test against its competitors, early in 1968. In fact *C&D* rather summed the whole attitude up when they observed that one of the cars in the test, the AMC Javelin, despite better handling than its rivals, would never sell well unless it also went blindingly fast. Nobody buying these cars for the street was even faintly interested in handling, nor in stopping once they'd started. In 1968 the 'Cuda had been given an expanded range of Powerplant options, and the standard engine was now the 225 slant six, a 318 V8 rated at 230hp and the 383. In between came a 340ci lightweight V8 which was exclusive to Barracuda in the Plymouth range. It was this engine which had been fitted to the *Car and Driver* test vehicle, an engine which delivered 275hp, ran a standing quarter in 14 seconds at 99mph – shooting the car from standstill to 100mph in 14.5 seconds. Off the line it saw 60mph in 5.9 seconds and 80 in 9.7; this was the car whose brakes, remember, had been determined by *Car and Driver.'*

'68 was also the year in which one of the musclecar legends made its debut with a name taken straight from a TV cartoon. The Plymouth Belvedere had demonstrated the classic heredity of the musclecar as it became the Belvedere GTX, the GTX and now the GTX Road Runner, soon to be simply Road Runner. Available as a hardtop or a coupe in its first year, it carried dummy hood scoops, special wheels, Road Runner nameplates and a cartoon bird decal on the sides and rear. It also had two engine options, and shoehorned under the hood was either the 383 engine with manifolds and heads from the 440 or the genuine article – the 426 hemi. Oh yes, and a horn which went 'beep-beep.'

By now the musclecar was five years old, and most things which could be done had been done. The hemi had been out on the street already, but somehow it found its rightful home in the Road Runner. *Motor Trend*, before they got around to voting it their Car of the Year, which they did in 1968, called it 'the simplest, starkest, most brazenly pure, non-compromising super car in history,' and they were speaking of the 383 with 440 heads and intake manifold. And while fans of some of the more exotic Italian machinery may have felt like arguing with the *Motor Trend* superlatives there was no doubt at all that the Road Runner was indeed something special. The starting point was the basic Belvedere body and a complete lack of luxuries, with

Left and below: The Satellite was yet another in Plymouth's muscle lineup. This was the company which entered further into the spirit of the thing to a far greater degree than most others.

the emphasis on performance. And, outside of traditional musclecar marketing techniques, Plymouth weren't shooting for a price, they gave the Road Runner everything it needed and let the price come out wherever it might. Altogether a bold technique, it paid off handsomely, since the basic 383 was only a few hundred dollars off the pace, although a few hundred dollars could buy quite a lot in this year when Julie Andrews was making the first version of Star!, Dick Van Dyke starred in Chitty Chitty Bang Bang, Otis Redding's *The Dock Of The Bay* went to number one after the plane crash which killed Otis and his band, the Bar Kays, and *I Heard It Through The Grapevine* occupied the number one spot for three weeks for Marvin Gaye.

For these few hundred dollars came the heavy-breathing 383, a handling package with anti-sway bar, heavy-duty shocks, huge torsion bar and heavy rear leaf springs. And although *Motor Trend* clearly loved the car to death even they were forced to concede that all that extra springing still couldn't compensate for the weight of the engine; the eternal compromise between ride and hand-

Above right: The 440 six-pack, heart of the Road runner.
Above: This cartoon bird is what the beep-beep was all about.
Below: Still looking reasonably modest, although the rear wing (**far right**), which was part of the NASCAR aerodynamic package, was becoming fashionable.

Above: Later in life, the Barracuda sheds its 'Son of Valiant' image and becomes a regular part of the Plymouth muscle stable.

the GTX and the Road Runner was replaced by incredible drawings. There were also some odd attempts to pander to the disciples of Timothy Leary, high priest of the love generation, currently following his advice to 'tune in, turn on and drop out' all over America but especially in San Francisco's Haight-Ashbury.

Barracuda, having been advertised heavily with wide black sidestripes enclosing the 383 motif and looking altogether very tough indeed, suddenly gained a new option. Called a mod top, it replaced the usual paint or vinyl

ling had been made and (as usual) had come down in favor of a comfortable ride. Even wide tires couldn't completely disguise the fact that the 383 could hurl the 3660 lbs of Road Runner around at frightening speed. The brakes were huge 11-inch drums front and rear, although there were disks available for the front – as an option.

By 1969 those dummy hood scoops had become a real cold air induction system called Air Grabber on the GTX and Coyote Duster in the Road Runner. You have to watch the cartoons to know why. Plymouth were certainly showing that they had a sense of humor; they were using it in some of the most over-the-top advertising ever as well, as magazine spreads for the 'Rapid Transit System' claimed that 'the beat goes on' and photographic representation of

Above: Even with the big-block V8 in place the engine compartment was still spacious enough.
Above right and right: Along with the wing and the beep-beep horn came a selection of decals.
Below: Shorn of wing and droop-snoot, the Road Runner was a good looker.

roof with a fabric stick-on in an interesting black and yellow floral pattern. Seats could be ordered to match should the peace-loving musclecar freak buying the car so decide. Later in the year this option was also available on Satellite hardtops but, luckily, not Road Runner.

If ever anything signaled the end of the era then the floral roof has to be the advance guard, a sign that all may not have been well. But even as the storm-clouds were gathering over the eastern horizon Plymouth were preparing for their greatest excesses and also a facelift for the Barracuda. Rushed onto the street to meet Mustang, it had been based on the Valiant all its life so far. Meanwhile Chevrolet had finally produced their own answer to the Mustang (and along the way a competitor for their own Corvette) and Barracuda's restyle was as much an answer to the now three-years-old and highly successful Camaro.

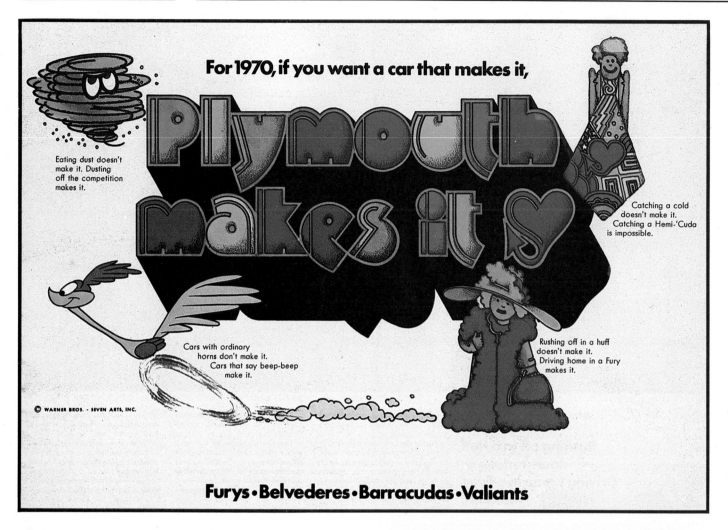

For 1970, if you want a car that makes it,

Plymouth makes it ♥

Eating dust doesn't make it. Dusting off the competition makes it.

Catching a cold doesn't make it. Catching a Hemi-'Cuda is impossible.

Cars with ordinary horns don't make it. Cars that say beep-beep make it.

Rushing off in a huff doesn't make it. Driving home in a Fury makes it.

© WARNER BROS. - SEVEN ARTS, INC.

Furys • Belvederes • Barracudas • Valiants

Sport Satellite

For those who won't put up with mundane motoring.

If you're looking for "plain-vanilla" transportation, you'd best look elsewhere. The Sport Satellite is anything but.

Is it really new? Let's just say it never existed before, and go from there.

The massive styling features high-curvature side glass. Full-length body accent stripes. And a flared, "hour-glass" look in the rear quarter panel area.

Power? Plenty. It starts with a standard 318 cu. in. V-8 and soars to an optional Super Commando 383 4-barrel — the latter with dual exhausts.

And here's a little clue to the kind of options available for '68.

AM radio/stereo tape setup artfully built into the instrument panel.

The name of the game this year is "sport." As in Sport Satellite.

SPORT SATELLITE HARDTOP. As you'll see at first glance, our stylists really put the squash on ordinary this year. Starting with the newly styled one-piece grille. Bright length wheel lip and sill moldings. Sporty full-length tape stripes (choose from 5 colors). And in back, brand new deep-recessed taillamps.

Then just to please every palate, we've added a rich Saddle Bronze Boar-Grain vinyl roof to the list of exterior options. (In addition to white, black, and antique green.) Now, remember when "regular gas" meant "plain car"? Sport Satellite has ended that notion once and for all. With a standard 318 cu. in. V-8 up front that lives on regular. And delivers the power where it really means something. On the open road.

But that doesn't mean you can't add more thrills and excitement. Ask for the 383 cu. in. 2-bbl. V-8. Or go all the way. With the Super Commando 383 4-bbl. V-8. Coupled with a floor-mounted Hurst 4-Speed Shifter. Unsilenced air cleaner. Heavy-duty suspension and 3.91 axle ratio. (You're back on premium now—a small price to pay.)

You might get the idea that Belvedere Sport Satellite's an exceptional car. You're right. Until you take a look at the low price tag.

Plymouth threw themselves into the muscle image wholeheartedly.
Their advertising was, without doubt, the most flamboyant of all.

Road Runner

Brilliant performance. Private property of the young and aware. Priced right.

Road Runner. It's what "out of sight" is all about.

It's side-opening hood scoops, like on GTX. It's dual exhausts. Heavy-duty suspension. Red Streak Wide Boots. Four on the floor, standard. And a standard engine so exclusive you can't even get it on another Plymouth.

It's called the Road Runner 383, has a 4-barrel carb. Performance cam. Dual exhausts. A newly developed cylinder head. Plus split-lip like a chrome oil filler cap, black crackle-finish unsilenced air cleaner, and 383 Road Runner engine emblem.

And get this. If you're a more the merrier type when it comes to engines, you can fit out Road Runner with the renowned Street Hemi. In fact, it's the only optional engine we'll equip it with.

For kicks, you get a Road Runner nameplate on the dash and deck lid. Another on the doors. Plus a cartoon Road Runner on the deck lid, the doors and on the instrument panel.

All this in a new 2-door coupe that's exclusive among Plymouth's competition. By giving it the same roof as our hardtops, you get frameless front door glass. And the rear windows tip out.

To make Road Runner even more of a good-times car, think about asking for options like the performance paint treatment. (A natty black patch between the hood scoops.) Or a vinyl roof. New easy-reading tach. Body paint stripes. Wide sill moldings. A special package including 3.55 rear axle with Sure-Grip, heavy-duty radiator and shrouded viscous-drive fan.

Oh, yes. The horn goes "beep-beep."

The Plymouth win-you-over beat goes on.

41

Muscle CARS

CHEVROLET

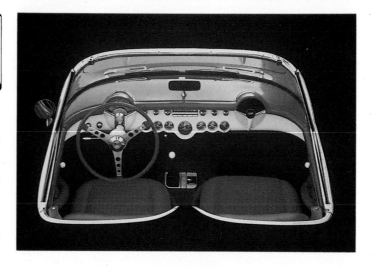

Chevrolet involvement in the musclecar phenomenon had begun in 1953 with the appearance of the Corvette as America's first 'real' sportscar aimed along traditional European lines. It was the first time any manufacturer had designed a car from the ground up with the intention of competing directly with the fleet-footed European imports. The only drawback to the Corvette program was the power-plant. Pretty, made out of fiberglass, designed along what were, for American cars, fairly revolutionary lines, Corvette was given a hopped-up version of the faithful stovebolt six to drag it around, coupled with two-speed auto transmission, and there was no doubt that America found it lacking.

It wasn't until 1955, and the advent of Chevrolet's new V8, that Corvette actually got any horns at all. The 265ci, 225hp smallblock which replaced the lowly 150hp of the 235 Blue Flame was fitted to a variety of cars, of course, including the classic Tri-Chevy sedans, and was readily adopted by the hotrodders as the slot-in option for racing, on the street or on the strip.

But it was in 1957, when the 283 V8 got injection, that things really began to move. Chevrolet had been working on the development of an injection system for some time, with little noticeable success, until this momentous engine. With a camshaft of startling duration and effect this engine developed one hp for each inch of capacity, which at the time was felt to be the optimum towards which engineers aimed.

The camshaft had been designed by an ex-racing driver who, like Carroll Shelby, had driven Porsche's Spyder to international wins before retiring from competition. No Texan, Zora Arkus Duntov was a Belgian-born Russian

Humble beginnings. The 50's Corvettes were hardly muscular. But they started a performance ball rolling at Chevrolet which kept the smallblock V8 at the top of the pile for decades. The 1960 (**above and above right**) showed its early pedigree, but, with fuel injection, was the fastest production car in America.
Below and below right: Bill Mitchell's split-window Sting Ray set the seal on Corvette muscle from 1963 on.

who gave the hotrodders the engine they'd been searching for and gave the Corvette some power to back up its good looks. Over the next few years Corvette became America's favorite sportscar, keeping the sleeker body which arrived in 1956 until Bill Mitchell's redesign in 1963. In between there was much more use of aluminum, and great attention paid to handling, especially by Duntov; he believed that every Corvette buyer should be presented with an article which was at its best on the racetrack. Strangely, despite improvements, Corvette fared only moderately well in circuit racing.

Then came Bill Mitchell's Sting Ray, a split-window sports coupe with the agressive appearance which would dominate the next few years. Better still, the new IRS

meant that Corvette could actually keep the 360hp of the 327 V8 on the road. Boring out the smallblock had been a hotrodding trick, and Chevrolet wasted little time in getting the engine onto the production line; injected, it gave the car a 14.5/102mph standing quarter and a top speed of 135mph. But, as everyone knows, there's no substitute for cubic inches, and the 427 big-block, Porcupine head, rat motor arrived in '66, gave 425hp out of one 4bbl Holley, produced 13.04/105mph in the standing quarter, a top speed of 135mph still, and 0-100mph in 12.8 seconds.

Typical of the entire breed, there were options, and along the way came aluminum heads, even full aluminum engines (the legendary ZL1) coupled as usual with a range of transmission and axle options which allowed buyers to order a shopping trolley or a track-ready race car with a top speed in the region of 180mph – roughly the same as a modern Formula 1 race car. Running to begin with on vast 11-inch drums, Corvette finally got the disks it needed in '65, and had brakes which were so good they outran the GM brake abuse course and were described by *Road and Track* as 'so good they're boring.'

And it was not only for Corvette that the new brakes were

Inset above and below: The Mitchell restyle for the 1963 Sting Ray gave us the body shape which most people now associate with the muscle era.
Main picture: Small changes only by 1965, and the convertible still more popular than the coupe.

needed; GM had been pushing some muscle around in other areas as well. In 1962 the restyled Impala, rapidly becoming the most popular model on sale in the USA, had changed from the eyecatching lines of the befinned '59 models to a crisp and workmanlike sedan. In 1962 it was given a performance option, and as Impala SS could be ordered with the big 425hp 409. Heavy-duty shocks, stiffer springs and sintered metal brake linings helped, as did the very quick power steering, but they were all needed; the 3700lb monster rode a 119-inch wheelbase and was the highest-powered Chevrolet so far to be offered.

But it was a big car, and the growing Federal regulations which surrounded it saw that its lifespan was short, and it disappeared in 1967. By then, though, it had matured to its full splendor, and was one of the most expensive models Chevrolet had yet offered, tempting *Car Life* to pose the question 'is a Chevrolet worth $5000?' The obvious answer to that was a big yes, since the Impala in question now sported a 427 V8 producing 385hp. Every one of which was well used, as the car sped to 100mph in 22 seconds and covered the quarter in 15.75/86.5mph. Not bad for a car which weighed in at over 4000lbs. And incredibly, *Car Life* found the brakes were desperately poor at any speed other than city cruising. The solution was simple; spend the tiny sum of $79 and get front disks which were unbelievably still optional. No wonder cars like this were beginning to attract displeasure from the government, and no wonder the super-powerful Impala program was cut short.

By the time it was canceled the big Impala musclecar had been well and truly replaced by a surprise entrant into

Top left: Big and heavy, the Chevelle SS carried the fabled 396 big block.
Left: The Impala, too, took big-block power in this 67 SS.
Above: Long after the period ended the big Chevy is a prized collector's car.
Bottom: The 396 engine, with later additions.

the big league – the mid-sized Chevelle. Introduced in 1964 to compete with Fairlane, the car which had given Ford their performance engine, the Chevelle was as roomy as the Impala but much smaller externally, having a 115-inch wheelbase. As a mid-range passenger car it was astoundingly successful and sales were plotted on a continually climbing graph. Very late in '65 – so late as to be little more than a marketing exercise aimed at upstaging the Mopar street hemi due in '66 – the muscle version of Chevelle was announced: the SS396.

The engine was the descendant of the Z-11 'mystery' engine which GM had debuted at Daytona in 1963, the 'semi-hemi' porcupine head which was later christened the rat motor. There was a bigger, 427 version of this engine, but it was only available in Corvette and full-size models in the Chevrolet range. The 396 Chevelle was offered in two levels of specification in which the part which made all the difference was the cam. Otherwise they were both single four-barrel jobs with 10.25:1 compression. In 1966 the hot one had 11:1 compression ratio (cr) and gave 375hp, but a drop in cr meant that by '66 it was down to 360, while the lower spec engine gave 325hp. Traditional by now was the stiff suspension and four-on-the-floor gearshift, but all Chevelles through the range had basically the same chassis and suspension, apart from convertibles. It was this stiffer frame which the SS models had originally been built on but which was now scrapped, making it lighter, more flexible and looser to drive. In 1966 Chevrolet also scrapped the rear sway bar, retaining it for the front only; like other makers they felt it was of limited value, although Oldsmobile and Buick continued to fit it, and

many testers felt that its absence was responsible for the floppy feeling at the rear end.

And incredibly, in '66, Chevy also dropped the big 11-inch drums which came from the full-size models and which had been on the '65 Chevelle, reverting to the 9.5-inch items standard on their mid-size cars. Early in 1966 *Motorcade* called that 'inexcusable regression,' and certainly Chevelle came in for some heavy criticism of a braking system which was now hopelessly inadequate for the task. It was a strange decision to say the very least, especially since safety was now one of Detroit's major headaches, as more and more Federal interest and regulations were being encountered. However Chevrolet did offer metallic linings as a highly desirable option. As *Motorcade* said 'we recommend them most emphatically to anyone considering the purchase of an SS396.'

In 1968, when Chevelle was available on two different wheelbase lengths (116 inches for the four-doors and 112 inches for the two-doors) it was also available as the SS396 or the 327 Malibu. The big musclecar was still suffering from the legacy of thrusting the vast big-block into a chassis which had never been designed for the task, and suffering badly. Externally the body had been revamped to give the long hood and short deck appearance which the Mustang had made fashionable, and also had the contemporary thick 'C'-pillars of the semi-fastback, but had problems lugging the big rat motor around. Altogether it made for a wallowy ride and handling of indeterminate accuracy, all of it conducted in a noisy and rather boomy bodyshell. Many people preferred the smallblock version. The lesser weight of the 327 made the Malibu a nicer and

Federal government. In the meanwhile, though, their strategy was right as far as the musclecar buyers were concerned, and Chevelle continued to sell well.

But that doesn't mean it got better. At the beginning of '69 *Car and Driver* ran a comparison test of six musclecars, which included a GTO, Road Runner, Mercury Cyclone and, of course, a Chevelle Malibu SS396. This was a 325hp 396, and the SS package now included power disks on the front. But, of all the cars they tested, the Chevelle went the slowest in the acceleration tests and was the most difficult car of all to bring to a stop. In fact *Car and Driver* said that Chevelle braking was 'barely acceptable' by their standards. Despite the fact that it compensated by having the best ride and also the best handling out of the six, *C&D* ranked it fifth. The 'unbeatable' handling, they said, was all down to the new heavy duty suspension package – which reintroduced that controversial rear sway bar which reduced understeer and held the car flat enough in cornering to give it the kind of directional stability which makes the driver feel comfortable. In fact Chevrolet had restored the Chevelle to the way it was when those few early models had been pushed through the line right at the end of '64.

Car and Driver made one other major observation, based on the fact that Chevelle was now the quietest of the six cars tested, and said that the exhaust design – now minus the horrid air injection pump - may well have been a definite improvement. Sluggish though it was, they found the test car quicker than they had expected, despite the fact that significant items of emission control equipment had begun to appear on all engines, especially those destined for California.

Also, noted *C&D*, the Chevelle was quicker than another model in the Chevrolet lineup; one which was fitted with the same engine and should have been well out in front since it was meant to be GM's principal Mustang-basher. Introduced to great acclaim in 1967, the Camaro was already found wanting.

Above left: Restyled again for 1968; Corvette was still the GM flagship.
Bottom left: 1972, and the low-compression engines were just a breath away.
Below: The eighties answer – the multiple-carb V6.

easier car to drive, especially in tight curves. Which was bad news for owners of the 396, because the extra 100hp (375 over 275) meant that the big SS was noticeably quicker, making 0-100 in 15 seconds instead of 30 and covering the drag racers' quarter-mile in 14.8/98.8mph rather than 16.8/82mph. Clearly there is a contradiction visible, and again common to many of the musclecars, in that conventional auto design dictates that the faster a car goes the better it should handle and stop; certainly better than lower-powered vehicles. And although the SS stopped faster and more often without fade than the Malibu, *Car Life* described the brakes on the SS396 as good, with moderate control loss, while they rated the Malibu as very good, with only slight loss of control. All of which meant that Chevrolet were deliberately marketing a car which was both faster and more ponderous than similar models of their own manufacture. Nor were they alone, and it was precisely this attitude which was attracting the attention of

CAMARO

The Chevrolet Corvair, which had all the right ingredients to be a long-lasting supercar, but in the wrong order, was ailing badly by the mid-'60s. It had got off to a bad start, with an overweight flat six motor which engineers agreed had what they termed a 'negative effect' on the car's handling. By the time the engine had been bored out to give it some zip and the rear swing axle – never a good idea for cars with a pronounced rearward weight bias – had been replaced, things were already too late. Ralph Nader's book *Unsafe At Any Speed* was already having a noticeable effect on sales and the lawsuits claiming that the car was intrinsically dangerous weren't helping either. It would be ten years before a congressional investigation settled the matter in Corvair's favor, but by then it would be too late.

More damaging still was the arrival of the Mustang, against which the Corvair could not compete in performance terms. In any case volume sales on that sort of scale were out of the question since the Corvair was an expensive car to build. The Mustang had to be met head-on by a conventional front-engine sportscar, and responsibility for

designing it went to Bill Mitchell. Under him GM Art & Design came up with a car which was similar to the Mustang – low roofline, long hood, short deck, flat nose, flat tail – but a little more elegant.

More importantly, GM borrowed the option list from the Mustang and the Camaro came with 81 different factory options and 41 dealer-installed accessories which would allow buyers to tailor their new car to an exact but personal specification. As ever the base engine was a straight six of some 140hp, a more powerful version of the same, the 327 V8 and, exclusive to Camaro in this first year, the 302 V8 and the 350 smallblock.

It was this smallblock which would become firstly a favorite among Corvette owners and eventually the GM standard issue for all models of everything, but the 302 was just as interesting. In the first place GM were officially no longer involved in racing of any sort, yet the new engine just sneaked the car into the Group 2 sedan class of racing, which had a top limit of 305ci. More interestingly it was this engine which formed the basis of the Z-28 package which was available at Chevrolet dealers for street use, which was – and remains – the most performance oriented Camaro of them all.

In order to get hold of the 295hp 350 buyers had to check the SS option on the order blank and thrown in with the engine their $211 got them a stiff suspension package,

All-new for 1967, the Camaro had one of the longest option lists in Detroit and was Chevy's Mustang-basher in Rally Sport trim (**top**), as straight SS 350 (**above**) or SS 350 convertible (**left**).

wide oval tires, extra sound insulation, SS emblems and some striping on the hood. Later on in the year came the real performance option, though, when $400 bought the 396 big-block and the Turbo Hydra-Matic. There were also metallic brake linings, power disks, power brake booster, power steering, high ratio manual steering, positraction, an assortment of rear axle ratios and a lot more.

But the option game wasn't only played with hardware, and there were three different types of steering wheel available, as well as shoulder belts, headrests, tinted glass, a clock, airconditioning, five different types of wheel; and wheel cover, aluminum rocker panels, black-painted rocker panels and different seats and interior trim. It was easy enough to lift the base price of $2466 to well over $5000 just by ticking the right boxes, and the Camaro was available in more guises than any other single car in production at the time.

Yet again there was a noticeable difference in ride and handling between models with the smaller engine and those with the big V8, and many testers felt that the straight sixes rode and handled far better than those carrying the V8 up front. But then performance was a compensation, and the straight six Camaros had a top speed of only 104mph, ran the quarter in 18.5 seconds at 75mph, against 120mph flat out from the larger SS350 and quarters at 15.8/89mph. And that was the larger, 250-inch six.

Which is probably a good reason for offering 9.5-inch drum brakes as standard, although *Car Life* found them wanting, as they were on all the Chevy products *CL* had tested. Performance options included either front disks or a power booster or metallic linings, although the Z-28 package included the power booster, heavy duty front

disks and metallic rear linings all together, which must have been very useful for all those unofficial Camaros which went racing.

In fact there was considerable reason to believe that the existence of the roadgoing Z-28 was nothing more than a homologation exercise aimed at the FIA rules about Trans-Am racing, which required that, to qualify, there must be a minimum of 1000 cars generally available. A major reason for suspecting this was the involvement of Vincent Piggins; a veteran competition engineer, the Z-28 concept was his, and it was his engine design which made the car what it was. The 302 engine used the 327 block with a (forged) crankshaft from the 283, another long-duration camshaft, limited-slip diff, a range of final drive ratios, and a whole host of dealer-installed options like tuned headers.

Chevrolet rated the engine at 290hp at 5800rpm, but *Road and Track*, testing a Z-28 in mid-1968 found their best shift point for the four-speed box was around 7000rpm; the engine would handle it at 7500, but the

clutch wouldn't. Their opinion at the time was not that GM were lying about the power output but rather that they were only telling part of the truth. 290hp at 5800 may have been correct, but *Road and Track* felt that 350 at 6200 was just as true and realistic, as well as far more revealing. *Road and Track* concluded that the Z-28 was untractable, lumpy at idle and rumbled a bit as did most of the musclecars fitted with a handling package. Unlike the bulk of them with the low-size engine option the Z-28 was very quick; 140mph-plus top speed and 14-second quarter-mile times. Their conclusion was that 'Chevrolet had obviously achieved what they set out to do — build a race-winning Trans-Am sedan.'

They weren't all that wrong, either. Soon after its introduction the Z-28 beat the Mustangs at the end of the '67 season and came home first and second in the Trans-Am class of the '68 Sebring 12-hour race. It was class champion in the Trans-Am Series in '68 and in '69, winning 18 out of 25 races. It was only after those victories that Chev-

From the SS 350 (**inset**) came the Camaro competitor for Trans Am races — the Z28 (**main picture**).

rolet wished or became bold enough to market the Z-28 strongly. It had been there in '67, lurking in the option boxes, but in '68 it was being sold as the GM 'mean streak,' and even came with four-wheel disks borrowed from Corvette as one of the options, although most of the racing parts were now only available as dealer-installed, and remained relatively obscure and rare.

There were two camshafts available for the Z-28, but one of them was so wild that it would have been totally impractical on the street; nothing very much at all happened below 4000rpm. Even without it stock 302 engines with nothing more than a blueprint had pulled close to 400hp on a dynamometer, and the Z-28 really made use of its close-ratio Muncie gearbox, but Chevy still stuck to that 290hp rating. Anyone who drove one, on street or strip or track, knew the truth.

And there soon were large numbers of people driving their Z-28 on the street. Originally a numbers game for the FIA, a mere 600 of them were built in 1967, but there were 7199 the following year and 19,000 in 1969. The same sales success wasn't for the Dana 427, though. Essentially a private development, it was nonetheless born out of the power struggle between Camaro and its target, the Mustang. Originally launched with the 350 as its top engine option, Camaro grew a 396 after Ford announced the 390 Mustang. Then, as part of the Shelby arrangements, came the GT500 with the vast 428 engine. Chevrolet made no comment, nor any changes to its lineup, but a Chevy dealer from California, Dana, slipped the Corvette 427ci 425hp motor into Camaro and offered it for sale. On top of the base 350SS package Dana added the big motor, Muncie four-speed, Positraction rearend, metallic brakes, tuned headers, heavy-duty clutch with an NHRA scattershield and a selection of extra instrumentation. And even Dana, on the ultimate performance Camaro, offered disk brakes as an option.

Below: The 1970 Camaro facelift made it sleeker still. This car has the optional Rally Sport equipment.

The 427 needed them. Top end was 130, acceleration to 100mph was a mere 14 seconds, and the measured quarter mile disappeared in 14.2/102mph. Credit to the factory, though; the 427 was only marginally quicker than the Z28 but handled worse. The extra engine weight of the 427 made the car understeer, and even the beefed up SS package was no help. Race winner though it was, the Camaro was never built to carry the huge mass of metal over its nose and sagged heavily; no amount of racebred heritage could save its handling from the same fate as every other musclecar which was given a vast engine never meant for it, thrust into a chassis never designed to take it. Although the performance was blistering in a straight line, turning corners was never easy.

Chevrolet's non-involved attitude to racing had a curious effect on hard parts for their sporty and musclecars. While Ford were still deeply committed to Total Performance and would spend money on any development for the track, Chevrolet could not — unless whatever parts were developed from it were made available as performance or heavy-duty options to their customers. This meant that you could buy any trick part for your Camaro in any of Chevy's 6000 US dealerships almost as soon as it had proved its worth on a racetrack somewhere; you had to be able to do that so the budgeting could be justified to the GM accountants. But outside of the limited range of bits which Ford made available through Total Performance there was nothing for Mustang owners.

All of which was decidedly contrary to the spirit, if not the letter, of the GM 'no racing' edict. In the end it would be the gas crisis, not the internal memorandum, which would shut down this active participation, and the Z-28 would be no more. The name was not created, it was taken from the order blank, where a tick in box number Z-28 bought the 302 with all the fast bits. Later, long after the reality of the fast bits was gone, Chevrolet would use the nostalgic association of the Z-28 name as a tool to sell a low-compression plodder, a Camaro with a progressively decreasing power output.

NOVA

As World War II ended Chevrolet looked to the future with designs for a rear-engined car known at the time as the Cadet. It eventually made production as the ill-starred Corvair, and proceeded to fail badly in the small-car stakes. Studebaker's Lark, the first modern compact, did so well that it brought the company a temporary respite, staving off the final crash. Chrysler swung the Valiant into the field and Ford relied on the successful Falcon to cover their share of the compact market. Initially GM relied on the Corvair in this market but it soon became clear that Corvair's non-traditional layout made it a favorite only among enthusiasts. The bulk of the market leant heavily towards a front-engine, rear-drive boxy sedan, and the way that Falcon was cleaning up was ample proof. As a stopgap GM fought the opposition with tame Vauxhall-Opel imports while they rushed their own domestic-built compact into production, and the Chevy 11 was created in 1962 offering either a four-cylinder or six-cylinder option on a 110-inch wheelbase.

By 1963 the Chevy 11 was outselling Falcon, no mean achievement and perhaps also no small indictment of the discerning requirements of the average car buyer of the time. But 1963 was the last year that Chevy 11 did well, and part of the reason was competition from the runaway success of their own Chevelle, a slightly larger vehicle which filled the gap left by the classic '55-'57 models. Chevy 11 received a number of marketing boosters, not least of all the well-tried SS packages, although in this case they were little more than badgework and trim changes.

So, in 1968, the Chevy 11 got a new body on a 111-inch wheelbase, and a change of name; it was now simply the Nova, previously the designation of the top-of-the-range Chevy 11. Sales were over 200,000 in 1968, making it the best year since 1963, and a strong advertising campaign kept it selling well. Competitive pricing, mainly down to the fact that it was only available in two body styles, was no small advantage either.

The optional V8 (the 283) had been available in 1964, and although it did little to aid sales (10,000 that year), it provided a hint of the performance capability of the car

Below: Chevy 11 was created in 1962 as GM's compact, and later became the Nova, getting its own SS designation to go with the performance engines. This 66 has a 327.

which the future would see realized. Despite the no-race ban, a Chevy 11 won its class in the Shell 4000 Rally that year.

The next season saw Chevy 11 go one step up the Chevrolet performance ladder, and although the six-cylinder 120hp Hi-Thrift was the standard powerplant, the newly-launched SS package had a number of options which now included a 300hp 327 V8. The SS options, as was normal across the Chevy range, also allowed for a floor-shift, Positraction rearend, heavy duty clutch, special suspension front and rear, plus sintered metallic brake linings and a brake booster.

There was a smallish facelift for 1966, making Chevy 11 somewhat less boxy than it had been, but more interesting was the addition of yet another engine to the range as last year's Chevelle option, the 350hp Turbo-Fire 327 V8, became available. This gave the car a 0-60 time of around seven seconds and allowed for quarter-miles in fifteen, making this small car no slouch at all. Amazingly, brake options for this 350hp brute were limited to sintered linings for the standard 9.5-inch drums fitted across the range, beginning with the 90hp/four, and magazine testers, beginning to enjoy the power and handling mix of the big engine in the small chassis, were progressively more and more disturbed by the horrific lack of braking capability.

The technique of putting big engines in little cars was owed almost completely to hotrodding. Chevrolet had proved over and over that they had no objection to borrowing a good idea, and the 283, 327 and finally 350-inch overbores on their own smallblock had first been done by weekend racers. Making this sort of power available as a factory package was the entire musclecar ethos and it worked in a minor way for Chevy 11, as '66 production went up above 20,000. But Chevy 11 hardly qualified as a musclecar, even with the 350; or if it did, it was a surprise entrant. It seemed to catch Chevrolet themselves unaware, and they were never quite sure what to do about it.

Their ambivalent attitude was exemplified in 1967; there were no real styling changes after the '66 facelift because the big change was scheduled for '68. But the 350 and 300hp engines were dropped from the range completely,

Above and below right: Hood scoop, suspension modifications and race decals are modern additions to Chevy's famed Nova SS streetfighter.

and replaced as top power option by a 275hp version of the 327. Sales were back down to the 10,000 mark, and the restyle was just in time to save it from cancellation.

The '68 models were slightly bigger and heavier, swoopier and more curvy, but not as neat as their predecessor. Nonetheless they were right on the button for current market needs. Owing much to the styling of the successful Chevelle, the Nova was a definite lookalike to those not too interested or not looking too closely; you could buy Nova and kid people you'd spent money on the bigger car. In 1968 more than 200,000 people did; an incredible jump from the previous year.

But there was also something else; something quite unusual for a car this little – the top performance option for the '68 Nova was the big-block 396 engine. And not just the stock 325hp 396, but the monster 375hp version. There were a large number of differences between the two motors which accounted for that 50hp jump. The 375 had a heavy-duty block with 4-bolt mains, a heat-treated forged crank, strong alloy conrods, long duration, high-lift cam, forged pistons, high performance heads with huge ports and valves, a hi-capacity aluminum intake manifold and an enormous 800cfm Holley double-pumper to set the whole thing off. That summer *Car and Driver* arranged to test a Nova equipped with all the goodies. The fully-loaded cars were so rare that an experimental model, on which GM engineering were studying the cooling system, had to be borrowed from the Tech Center and tested in Detroit. *C&D* evinced no qualms about giving this sleeper a workout along Woodward, in the firm belief that most people would simply write it off as a Nova, and they thought they could surprise and embarrass large numbers of youthful muscle drivers. They were wrong. Apart from the low-restriction exhausts, which produced a rewarding and exciting rumble, the understated SS 396 badges were seen and recognized by everyone in Detroit under the age of 25 and all policemen everywhere, regardless of age.

In a frighteningly short timespan the Nova SS had

gained itself an awesome reputation as a street killer, and no wonder. This was true rocket-sled performance, only fractions of a second behind Chevy's own supercar, the 400hp Corvette. On the graph the performance curve was all but vertical and acceleration figures just as impressive to quote: 0-30mph in just 2.2 seconds, 0-60 in 5.9, 0-100 in 14.3 and standing quarters 14.5/101mph. And this from what was ostensibly Chevrolet's big-selling family compact. Moreover, *C&D* said that the Uniroyal tires on their test car were little short of appalling and accounted for the rather poor results in the acceleration tests!

They also had a car with the 3.55 street rearend, and the last yards of the quarter put the car into fourth, where a better ratio would have held on longer and given a noticeable time advantage. Along the same lines was the observation that as the car warmed up the quarters got slower in response to increased temperatures under the hood; a fresh air package (already an option on Camaro and others) could also have improved on what were already very good times.

And while they admired the light-to-use experimental dual-plate clutch on their test car (due on the production line from 1969 onwards for everything with 350ci and over), they found some things to complain of. While the Muncie box was admirable the shift linkage never was, and they described the dash as 'a masterpiece in the great Chevrolet tradition.' While basic instrumentation (like speedo and clock) were well-placed, there were no other sources of information other than warning lights which, observed *C&D*, 'only serve notice that you should speak of your engine in the past tense.'

But while these faults were decidedly incorrect, the most serious criticism was reserved again for the braking system, or rather the lack of one. The test car did have a front disk/rear drum arrangement, but as with many GM models, even when they worked adequately the suspension let the car down, producing a hopping at the rear end

which made it difficult to control the car during braking and a test of nerve to keep the pedal firmly pressed. Even on the test track *Car and Driver* found that this combination 'brings a certain verisimilitude to a panic stop.'

Weight distribution was not to blame; 55 percent sat over the front, a ratio which was at least as good as some of the sporty cars and a whole lot better than one or two of them. In fact Nova handling was a delight, and, for example, provoked none of the adverse criticism aimed at the Camaro when front-loading it with the big-block motor produced sloppy understeer and wallowing nosedives. Stiffer front springs carried the extra weight of the big-block, and the extra understeer so induced was balanced out by negative camber; fast-ratio power steering still allowed the driver to feel the road and was generally held to be a long way in advance of anything yet offered by Ford.

The Nova's braking problem was probably in the rear suspension arrangements; leaf springs can be made to work, and work quite well, but they didn't in the Nova. *Car and Driver*'s tester found it hard to believe that 'any government-fearing corporation would make a car with this problem available to the public.' Overall, though, the Nova was highly rated by the people it was aimed at; the musclecar enthusiasts. Even the *Car and Driver* testers took it along Woodward at night, crawling round the lot at Ted's Drive-In, looking for action. Not only did they get no takers from the young streetracers gathered there, but they were immediately told by the police to park or move on.

By '69 the list of options for under-the-hood entertainment had increased even further, as the 350 from the Camaro range became available to Nova buyers, along with the 307 V8. Around the 400-inch mark Chevrolet engines began to get very confusing, especially since all the options were open to Nova buyers. They could have the 375hp 396 big-block, or the 325hp 396 big block, but the important thing to remember is that neither of them were 396 any longer; they were both 402. They were called 396 to avoid confusion with the other 402 (which was called the Turbo Jet 400) and the Turbo-Fire 400 – which really was 400ci but was an overbored smallblock, not a big-block like the rest of the big-inch family.

The big engines were definitely useful; even as a compact the Nova weighed in at over 3500lbs, which meant that the full-house 375hp unit was the only engine which allowed it to compete with the much lighter ponycars on anything like equal terms. However the 350 was the popular option, as the bulk of Nova production went to family buyers who found the 250hp of the soon-to-be-standard smallblock more than adequate. Even in this bracket there were practically no takers for the 90hp in-line four, and few for the 155hp six; the Nova was a heavy car for such tiny powerplants.

And even though the little four-pot would soon be deleted as too feeble, so too the big-inch engines would be cut as too powerful, too thirsty and too dirty. Horsepower advertising would soon be banned, and low-octane, unleaded gas would see the end of the high compression engines. Although Nova itself would continue until replaced by the front-drive Citation in '79 the big-block days were over almost as soon as they had begun.

AMERICAN MOTORS

Kenosha, Wisconsin, is perhaps an unlikely address for manufacturers of a big musclecar range, but it is just that. Just outside Detroit, it's also a somewhat apt address for a maker continually just outside the biggest of big leagues, sometimes known as one of the Big Four and other times way down the list. The American Motors Corporation manufactured vehicles at Kenosha with some notable success, not least of which was the highly individual Nash Metropolitan, which was also sold under the Hudson nameplate for a short while before the make was discontinued. But their big success story arrived in the late fifties on a 108-inch wheelbase carrying a compact economy sedan. All traces of Nash and Hudson were removed from this model, and the car was sold as a Rambler.

By 1961 the success of the Rambler had raised American Motors to third place in the sales league; an unparalleled achievement for an independent, selling half a million cars and leaving big names like Plymouth and Pontiac behind. But the success of Rambler was its own undoing, since it signaled the start of a rash of compacts from the big three which soon pushed AMC back down the league, until they were 12th by 1967.

Back in 1957 Rambler had released a model based on their Custom, known as the Rebel. Their 250ci V8 had been introduced in that year, giving 190hp at a lowly 4900rpm, and the Rebel was now given an oversquare version which produced a healthier 255hp, and pushed the car from rest to 60mph in around seven seconds. However it did not particularly appeal to Rambler buyers, most of whom fell into the sort of mold at which the generally more staid compacts were aimed. With heavy-duty Gabriel shocks, sway bar, uprated springs, power steering and power brakes the Rebel carried a specification which was ahead of its time in many ways and also way out in front on price. The most expensive car in the range; it did not sell well, and only about 1500 of them were built.

As the compacts began to set records for AMC the Rebel vanished, and would probably have stayed vanished had not the arrival of the Mustang prompted the AMC Marlin and launched AMC into the musclecar market proper. The Rebel badge reappeared when the Rambler Classic, introduced in '61, was facelifted and renamed in the 1966 model year and from then on AMC treated it as a make in its own right.

The V8 which powered the first Rebels was an old Hudson design, although by the early sixties it had jumped to 270hp, and it was this engine which was slotted in when the Rebel returned; by '67 the 327 had been stroked to 343 and was delivering 280hp, although much of the work on this engine had been done for the Marlin, launched with a 327 V8 as an answer to the Fairlane smallblock in the Mustang.

Although styling on the Marlin (a reworked Rambler Classic with huge curving areas of glass leading into the fastback rear) was reasonably adept, and lent the car the appearance of being a competitor for Mustang, the 327 V8 in that initial year did nothing of the kind. Its 0-60 was 12 seconds, and it took the standing quarter at a gentle 18 seconds/76mph, which was hardly likely to generate the kind of G-Force or excitement which was supposed to be the musclecar prerogative.

In '66 the Rambler designation was dropped for the Marlin, and it joined Rebel under the AMC classification, proving conclusively that badge engineering was not the sole preserve of the big three. It also indicated that AMC were deeply anxious to break into the growing musclecar market, and they began to offer the 343ci 'Typhoon' 4bbl V8 as an option on a range which included Ambassador, Rambler American (as it was now called) as well as Marlin and Rebel. The big-engined Rebel was known as the SST, although Concorde had yet to make the initials part of everyday language. Although it lifted the performance into a somewhat higher bracket, it still wasn't exactly blistering; 17 second quarters aren't the fastest ever recorded among the competition. But AMC followed traditional lines, and speed packages were available. The three which helped most were a high-lift, long-duration cam which came with competition lifters and heavier valve springs; a 4.44:1 rear axle and a cold air system. All were available through AMC dealerships, and although early SST exhausts were single

Introduced in 1965 (this is a 66), the Rambler Marlin was AMC's answer to the Mustang, although not notably successful.

pipe the later ones came with a dual setup which improved the back pressure situation considerably.

This really only represented a small step in the right direction, and the go-faster goodies were nowhere near as sophisticated as the add-ons which other factories were making available; for example there were none of the hi-rise manifolds and multi-carburetor setups which typified the bulk of the big three output. And although the SST heavy-duty suspension gave it a noticeable handling advantage over the rest of the AMC cars without it, this again was not as effective as the musclecar buyers had grown used to from other factories and by now felt, quite properly, they had the right to expect.

What AMC had tried to do with their range – as with the straight-six Rebel and the V8 Rebel SST – was to produce economy sedans and sporting machinery on the same line, using the same chassis and many of the same components. It was a technique which had been successful for Ford, Dodge and Chevrolet, but which AMC had failed to master. Quite simply, the SST was not muscly enough for the musclecar market.

The obvious next step was to put the big V8 into an even smaller car, and the Rambler Rogue (the smallest produced at AMC) was next to get the treatment. Even then, even with the wild cam, and even though AMC were reti-

Above left and right: The AMX set the seal on AMC's admission into the musclecar league.
Below: The Javelin SST was the car which gained them admission in the first place.

cent on the subject of horsepower so as not to offend the insurance companies, performance was still less than ex- hilarating, as the combination produced a 20-second 0- 100mph time and disappointing quarters at 15.8/88mph – marginally faster than the SST but still not in the same bracket as the real fliers in the same market. As a com- pensation the handling was more than fair, although mar- red by numb steering, and the front power disk/rear non- assisted drum setup provided excellent braking. But taken overall the Rogue was still not the car which would lift AMC into the big league or incidentally, out of financial prob- lems.

The car which would do that for them was announced in late '67 and was therefore a '68 model – the Javelin. Much

All pictures: The Javelin changed little in appearance and gained little in the way of performance. AMC didn't really have a big enough operation to give it the kind of back-up the musclecars needed to sell well.

better looking than the Marlin, it was a true Ponycar looka-like, with the Mustang's long hood and clipped rump, with no single panel of flat window glass to be seen; it was the kind of shape which is now accepted as 'Coke-bottle.' In SST form it was fitted with the 343 V8, a 280hp engine which seemed to fall in the middle ground somewhat. With 50hp more than the Mustang's 302 and 50 less than its 390, it fell well below the 325hp GM 327 smallblock and far behind the 385hp of the 427 big-block introduced the previous year. What it did conveniently match almost ex-actly was the 295hp of the new 350 smallblock now power-ing the Camaro and the Nova.

Javelin ran to 100mph in 17 seconds and the quarter 15/93mph although it may have done better with different tires and certainly would have done better with different ratios in the gearbox. All the testers of the time found them far too close together, and in their acceleration test in late

'67 *Car Life* spent only 1.5 seconds in second gear, picking up only 11mph before the shift into third. They found that they could produce quarter times which were almost iden-tical to the best-ever 15.4 seconds run they achieved if they ignored first completely and started the run in second.

There was another drawback in the power stakes as well, and that was purely down to AMC's size – or lack of it. Anywhere in America, from one of six thousand deal-erships or an unlimited number of private performance shops, you could get speed parts for GM cars, whether Corvette, Camaro or Nova. From Shelby you could buy an amazing range of things for Mustangs, and from Ford's Total Performance Program, or Plymouth's Rapid Transit System there were innumerable add-ons. AMC simply did not have the size, the structure, the personnel or the financing to provide the same kind of backup for SST buyers beyond the two or three dealer-installed kits for

camshaft and so on. Without those extras no Javelin could be as competitive in sport as any seriously modified car from the big three.

Despite this *Car Life* – and the bulk of the press – approved of the Javelin; AMC had dabbled with the musclecar market and had now made a bold and concentrated effort to move into it wholeheartedly – a brave decision for a company in as much financial hardship as AMC were well known to be. But the move paid off, and Javelin sold 56,000 units in the first year, outselling its Marlin predecessor by more than ten times.

The Javelin received minor bodywork modifications for 1969, but only a few since its styling was already clean and lean; in fact it was judged by many to be far superior in appearance to Mustangs and Camaros generally. It also gained some competition from its home stables; emboldened by its success AMC introduced another new model midway through '68, although the AMX, as the newcomer was named, was really only a smaller, two-seat version of

the Javelin, running a 97-inch wheelbase instead of 109 inches.

It looked like a sectioned Javelin as well, with a lump of bodywork simply removed from the middle, and the rest of the styling virtually identical; Javelin's short-chopped rear didn't sit well behind the truncated passenger compartment and the car looked rather odd in side view. AMC described the car as a 'Walter Mitty Ferrari,' and aimed it at a low-volume run; supplying limited specialist vehicles to markets ignored by the big three had always been their forte, and this is what they planned for this two-seat sportscar placed between the imports and domestic heavyweight ponycars, including their own Javelin. To say that AMX sales of 20,000 in three years were disappointing is partly true, since AMC were looking for 10-20,000 units per year.

What was big on the AMX was its new top-of-the-option-list 390ci, 315hp V8, which really supplied the kind of power levels the musclecar boys were looking for. This one gave it a 0-100 time of little more than 16 seconds and produced quarter times in low fourteens/high nineties, depending on the gearbox: the AMX came with four-speed manual or three-speed auto, and although the ratios were now sorted out the linkage wasn't, and unwary shifts produced variations in elapsed time and terminal speed.

The AMX fell midway between brackets, neither musclecar, ponycar nor sportscar.

It was also a heavy car, at 3200lbs, and with the 343 or 390 engines the heavy duty suspension, with a big front sway bar included, was a mandatory option. It was an option which worked well, and the AMX was a fairly nimble performer on twisty roads, with powerful and well-mannered brakes to match. It was, whichever way you look at it, basically a good car.

Naturally the big 390 found its way swiftly into the SST

Javelins, and in the course of time also under the hood of the Rambler Rogue, and it was in this guise, during 1969, that AMX began to use its musclecar operations like everyone else. The prime example was the SC/Rambler, the combination of efforts from AMC and Hurst Performance Products. Tricked up with all the stripes and badgework, with a manual floorshift which really worked, this was a typical example of the late sixties muscle mania; a small car with a large-capacity, high-output V8.

Rogue's adept handling, a power-boosted disk brake arrangement as standard and a quarter performance of 14 seconds/100mph, leading to a top end of around 115mph, made it a formidable contender on street and strip. And it came home well in front on price; at a fraction under $3,000 it was 30 percent less expensive than a hemi-equipped Road Runner.

The Javelins were doing well for themselves as well, especially in Trans-Am racing, turning in 0-60 in less than five seconds, quarters in 11 and top end clockings around 12's, although AMC still lacked the corporate structure to make the parts which turned the stock 390 SST into the Trans-Am racer available across the counter. However

MERCURY COUGAR

they'd got the message very clearly indeed, and in 1970 followed up on previous lessons with The Machine.

This started life as a Rebel 2-door hardtop, which was a semi-fastback with the braking and suspension beef-up kits as mandatory option. All this, plus the 390 with performance bits applied wherever possible brought it in at a heavy 3800lbs, which showed up noticeably in the figures. Standing quarters were mid fourteens/low nineties, and the suspension was hard (some might say harsh, although all agree that it worked very well), helping the high tail stance to make it harder to get real traction off the line as it added bounce to anticipated wheelspin.

340hp out of 390ci was acceptably high, although not as high as it might have been. On the other hand the engine was light and simple blueprinting produced measurable improvements. By now, of course, performance was getting to be a dirty word, and like everyone else AMC was reluctant to talk in horsepower numbers. In fact, they'd got themselves a bit of a problem all round, since here they were in 1970 with a car which was demonstrably a member of the muscle clique, loaded with matt hood bulging with cold air intakes, garish sidestripes, the tail-up stance of the dragstrip, even a hood-mounted tacho. And just as they finally became fully paid-up members of the big league it all began to fold up on them.

There's a theory in the auto industry that says when you see a gap in the market the one thing you don't do is devise a car which will fill it, because if it doesn't your whole range will be tainted by its failure. There's also the possiblity that if the gap is too far removed from the cars you are already selling the market itself may be unwilling to accept your product in a different role, and seal its fate that way. So what you do is create a whole new marque, basing your strategy on the belief that the average car buyer is too stupid to spot the connection.

It's a tried and trusted formula frequently known as badge engineering – which is what it always turns into – and it usually works quite well. Among other makes it has produced is Ford's Lincoln-Mercury Division, born in the late thirties out of Edsel Ford's belief that there was a gap beneath Oldsmobile which Pontiac weren't really filling. He was right, and Mercury got off to a good start, combining with Lincoln in 1947 to form a separate division along the lines of those operated successfully by GM.

An upgraded Mustang from Ford's Lincoln Mercury division, the Cougar's looks improve with the passage of time.

What this meant, of course, was that Lincoln Mercury took Ford products and moved them faintly upmarket in appearance, with styling changes and a longer wheelbase, making them look more luxurious and considerably more expensive even though they weren't. Although the breed did well there was never any question that it would approach the massive sales of its parent, though it was a consistent 12th or so in the sales league.

Postwar Lincoln-Mercury cars followed the same pattern as before, except that the decision to treat them as an autonomous make in their own right seemed to have gone rather by the board, and they filled in the Ford lineup wherever there was a gap, as the amazing variety of models, sizes, names and body styles through the early sixties shows. This apparently aimless marketing was also a reflection of and a contributor to the mixed fortunes of the division during the decade, although despite the confusion there were some cars which lasted most of the ten years, and Comet (in effect Mercury's Falcon), introduced in 1960, was still there in 1970.

Left: The engine bay, tidied up since 1967.
Below: Ford's own publicity material shows the Mustang heritage in Cougar's styling.

The Comet sold well at the beginning of its run and was boosted even further when, in '63, it became the only small Mercury offered, it did even better. The beginning of the sixties was also the start of the sporty compacts, and Mercury were soon offering options on the Comet; notably the S-22 two-door with the 101hp six. This car was re-named the Caliente in 1964 when the first facelift occurred, but by then performance options were burgeoning across the Comet range. Any car in the lineup could be given the 260 smallblock which was developed for Fairlane and there was also a slim-pillared hardtop coupe called the Cyclone which was aimed at the performance market and sported the 289 version of the V8 which was then good for 210hp.

The Comet had a major restyle in 1966, when it stopped being a compact and became an intermediate instead, based on a Fairlane shell and on the basis that Mercury buyers were well-off and would be happier with a bigger car for their money. It was not a decision which did well for Comet, and the name was gradually dropped from the lineup, although the Comet Capri, Comet Caliente, Comet Cyclone and Comet Station Wagon seemed to do quite well; it's just that the Comet designation was dropped from their name.

By 1967 Ford had been playing the performance game with Shelby for quite a few years, and high-performance versions of the smallblock were widely available. More interestingly, the big-block engines had also come into their own and were also available. Mercury, who had offered 390in, 335hp engines already, made use of them in '67, when the Comet Cyclone GT – which is basically just a flash Fairlane, remember – got the top-of-the-range big-block 427 which Fairlane was also awarded that year and which delivered either 410 or 425hp.

In this form the Cyclone was a champion streetracer and also no mean race car, pulling several titles on track and strip. This was partly down to the big engine, partly to the handy suspension which compared very well with almost anything on offer in a comparable bracket. It seemed, though, that perhaps not all of the knowledge from the Total Performance Program was being passed on to Lincoln-Mercury, as the Cyclone GT, basically an upmarket GTA Fairlane, received a less enthusiastic welcome from the press; it seems to have handled slightly less well – or perhaps just felt less solid and instilled less confidence, resulting in slower times – and did not incorporate many of the small features which made the GTA so popular. More to the point, the auto transmission carried upmarket ratios

designed for smooth cruising, and on the test track it kept changing gear at critical moments.

1967 also saw Mercury tack on to the Mustang sector of the market,or very nearly. Ford had, no doubt about it, vacillated for years, first chasing Corvette with T-Bird, then changing its character so much that when they needed to go after Corvette again ten years later they had to dream up a new name and invent Mustang. This time, instead of dropping the two-seater for a four-seater they decided to introduce the bigger car alongside. Now they needed a car which went into the range above Mustang but below the luxurious 'Personal car' which T-Bird had become, and they used Lincoln-Mercury to achieve it.

In 1967 they introduced the Mercury Cougar. Although it rode a 111-inch wheelbase, three inches more than Mustang, the Cougar was simply a luxury version of the successful Ponycar, and the two vehicles were mechanically almost identical under the skin. But outside was a different story, and the Cougar was truthfully a very pretty car. Maintaining the long hood and short deck, the body was restyled, sleeker and smoother than the Mustang, with concealed headlamps adding to the smoothness. The suspension was reworked to give a softer ride more in keeping with a bigger car, and masses of sound insulation was added to remove the musclecar rumble from the interior. While the Mustang's base engine was a lowly straight six, the Cougar started with the 200hp 289 V8, and moved through the V8 range all the way up to the Cougar GT package. Along with the 390 V8, the GT package involved a great deal of hardware which, on top of a revised suspension setup, included wide tires, special wheels, power brakes (with front disks) and other bits, which added to both safety and overall weight, making the now nose-heavy Cougar a less than outstanding performer in acceleration tests.

And then there was the luxury end of the market. To begin with this allowed the purchase of Cougars fitted with airshocks, special wheel covers, luggage carrier, ski carrier, a CB radio (long before anyone ever heard of CW McCall – or Burt Reynolds, come to that) and even a 9-inch TV set by Philips (who in those days were still called Philco). Then in February the XR-7, the real luxury Cougar was announced. Billed in the ads as 'America's first luxury sports car at a popular price,' the XR-7 was set up as direct competition to the fancy European imports, and many American press testers felt that the car compared reasonably well, although the opinion was not totally endorsed by European journalists.

The XR-7 had a mass of instrumentation set into a walnut dash, leather upholstery and an overhead console with map lights built in. Later there was the Dan Gurney Mercury Cougar Special, which rather than leaning towards Gurney's background, and being a really hot version of the Cougar, was nothing more than a bunch of cosmetics which included special wheel trims, a chrome engine dress-up kit and a Dan Gurney signature decal.

There were performance options though, and no wonder. The car was, after all, based on the Mustang, for which there was already a huge list of go-faster parts available over every Ford dealer's counter. Apart from the Cougar

GT, there was also the factory-installed Performance Handling Package, which was a set of high-rate springs all round, heavy-duty shock absorbers, large diameter sway bar, fast-rate steering and wide tires and wheels.

The whole Cougar range, while selling well, was never likely to catch Mustang up, but it did win *Motor Trend*'s approval, and became their Car Of The Year for 1967. There's another theory in the industry which says you shouldn't fool around with a winning formula, and the '68 Cougars were little different from the previous year – although they, like every other new car that year, bore the signs of encroaching Federal control as side marker lights and shoulder belts became compulsory. Emission controls were becoming compulsory as well, and most makers were fitting air injection pumps to their engines; low compression ratios and catalytic converters were just around the corner, but for now horsepower was still (just) acceptable.

Although Ford, perhaps for obvious reasons in view of the contemporary situation, made very little fuss about the advent of the 427 Mustang, the Mercury Cougar GT-E was treated to the full PR blast as Mercury used it to push performance as well as luxury. In fact the engine wasn't the fabled 'crossbolt' stock car item, but a detuned version with two-bolt mains, but it still pumped out a respectable 390hp, making it among the fastest of the ponycars ever made. Later that year the GT-E swapped its 427 for the easier to build but lower rated 428 Cobra Jet, which gave 335hp.

However hard it was pushed, the buyers didn't really make the connection between Mercury and muscle', and of the two different types of GT-E only 358 of the 427 and 244 of the 428 were built in the first year. Mercury generally was having a good time of things, and did better in '69 than they had in the ten previous years. The musclecar market was beginning its downward turn by '69, though, and Cougar sales reflected this quite plainly, despite the fact that this was a facelift year which also saw the introduction of a convertible.

The poor sales of the GT-E models meant that they were discontinued, but though the standard engine was the new 250hp 2bbl 351, and a more powerful 4bbl version giving 290hp was available as an option, the big 390ci engines were carried on, rated now at 320hp. There were also two 428 Cobra Jet engines, one with and one without the cold air induction system which Ford called Ram Air, although both were rated the same, at 335hp – yet another indication that establishment opinion was turning against the big cars and that the makers were concealing their true potential. The 375hp Boss 429, a regular option for Mustang buyers, was not on the list for the Cougar, although one or two did come through the factory gates.

Even in the face of the gathering stormclouds Cougar ran an extensive ad campaign throughout 1969, based on their newly-minted buzzword 'streep.' This was intended to represent a combination of the already commonplace 'street 'n' strip' appellation granted to high-power cars, and featured heavily in all press adverts, even though the division knew that the end of the era was all but on them. Even then they plugged on. The Eliminator show car – little more than a 428-engined Cougar with a trick paint job, was sold as an option in 1969 and again in 1970, although it was already scheduled for the ax in 1971. In a falling market the Eliminator held Cougar sales up, although it was small concession to the urgent need to boost sales; Chevrolet and Pontiac had restyled, Plymouth and Dodge brought out completely new models.

But in addition to fancy paint, Cougar buyers had the satisfaction of knowing that their 351 engines (or at least the bulk of the 2bbl and all of the 4bbl) were now Windsor-built, and although it appeared nowhere on the order blank, the Boss 429 and Boss 302 motors were also an option for Eliminator owners.

On a national basis the ponycar market was hardest hit of all in 1970; intermediates were the cars everyone bought. In 1971, then, the Cougar had its first real facelift, growing much wider and longer; it had become an intermediate. It had also lost most of its sporting image, the interior looked like the inside of any intermediate family sedan, and outside styling matched that feeling more or less perfectly. For Mercury at least, the musclecar was dead and gone.

The Cougar went through more 'special editions' than most, even at this period when Detroit was famous for it. This is the Cougar Eliminator.

BUICK

When plumber David Dunbar Buick decided to build cars and enter motor racing in 1903 he collected around him a team of fast, well-respected drivers which included the brothers Louis and Gaston Chevrolet. They did well: while sidevalve and T-head engines abounded, Buick used overhead valves, and the cars have never had anything else. It was more or less inevitable that Buick, constantly hovering on the financial edge of disaster, should need more capitalisation, and equally inevitable that eventually they should fall into the hands of the predatory William Crapo Durant. By 1908, after Dunbar's departure, Durant had formed General Motors out of Buick, Cadillac, Oldsmobile and Oakland.

By the forties Buick was GM's number two producer, right behind Chevrolet. Their lightweight ohv, 170hp, 322ci V8 (which, thanks to its pent-roof combustion chamber and central spark plug allowed only the use of very tiny valves and was christened 'nail-head' as a result) was introduced in their 50th anniversary year, 1953. The late forties and early fifties Buicks were among the most elegant cars of the period, thanks to Harley Earl's show cars like the Y-Job.

The first Skylark was another example of his excellent work, appearing in 1953 as a limited-run luxury sports convertible which sold for an amazing $5000. As the years went by the Skylark became less and less radical and also noticeably cheaper. Facelifts in the mid-fifties put Buick more or less ahead of Chevrolet in styling, and the '55 Riviera convertible was remarkably similar to Chevrolet's '57 Bel Air, and Buick passed through the tasteless period of heavily chromed toothy fronts and high, sweeping tailfins ahead of their stablemates, thus moving into the more refined design of the sixties sedans sooner.

As GM relied on the captive imports from Vauxhall-Opel to meet the demand for compacts which became evident during the mid-fifties Buick sold more Opels (which had been assigned to their division) than ever before, and to meet this growing need they redesigned their own lineup. Their compact emerged as the highly successful Special/Skylark of 1961, loosely based on the Corvair and powered by a lightweight aluminum V8 of 215ci which was boosted to 185hp in the Special Deluxe Skylark, which was more of a luxury tourer than a sporty car.

During the early sixties the big-block engine received a great deal of development work, gradually increasing in size up to the 1964 425. This engine was heavily used in competition and powered large numbers of full-size Buick models to dragstrip wins. As a dual 2bbl, it produced 360hp when supplied in the '65 Riviera Gran Sport, although there was a factory bolt-on kit with two 4bbl Carters available.

The 1965 Skylark Gran Sport, just one of the big Buicks to get the big-block treatment and the GS designation.

And it was the arrival of the Gran Sport designation which announced the arrival of Buick in the musclecar market. The Riviera Gran Sport with the dual quads was an impressive enough performer for its time, particularly since it was intended as a luxury tourer rather than a purposeful supercar. It was also regarded by many as the supreme example of Bill Mitchell's styling art, and possibly one of the best-looking cars of all time. It was also due in part to Mitchell's attempts to revive the LaSalle, which vanished in 1940, but was given to Buick as a sales tonic.

But on top of its good looks it was also a performer. It produced 0-100 in around 19 seconds and when the Super Turbine 400 gearbox was left in Drive it could run 15 second quarters – fully loaded with four passengers. And it carried them in impressive luxury which gave it a curb weight close to 4000lbs. It was not intended to be a small car, even though it was a lot shorter than the current crop of full-size Buicks.

It was clear that the engine performed extremely well in such a heavy car, and even clearer that as an option on the compacts it would do even better. The compacts had been restyled and lengthened over a 115-inch wheelbase in '64, and there were also a crop of new engines which included a 300ci V8. And by now the Skylark was emerging as Buick's best-selling compact, and it was only a matter of time before there would be a Skylark GS.

Apart from the 300ci engine there were also the Electra engines, 401ci big-blocks which were the Buick hotrod powerplants and made the full-size Wildcat the Buick performance model of the moment, up until the arrival of the Riviera GS.

In 1966 the Riviera grew to a 119-inch wheelbase and grew longer hood and fenders; the track was widened four inches to keep ride and handling at a comparable level. The headlights were concealed in the grille, and the GS package included heavy duty shock absorbers and a posi

By 1966 Buick had brushed up the image on Skylark and the other performance models, adding GS emblems and just a hint of hidden muscle.

Previous page: The 1966 Buick Wildcat. By now names were important, and 'Skylark' was hardly aggressive enough . . .
Above: But it stayed, and got tougher. This is the 1967 GS 400, with an obvious family resemblance to the more staid Electra (**below**).

rear axle as well as the 425 V8. Later the 425 option was changed for the Wildcat 465 motor. But for performance enthusiasts (as opposed to luxury buyers) this was overshadowed by the news that the Skylark had been allocated the Wildcat 401 power unit, running a single 4bbl as stock, dual exhausts and high-compression heads.

The shame was that it wasn't allocated some serious handling alternatives over stock; although the suspension geometry was quite good, the springing was soft and the car tended to wallow somewhat. Worse still, like all GM intermediates it was fitted with a two-speed auto gearbox; there was no performance option available, an incredible error in view of GM's own experience with the two-speed Corvettes at the beginning of the run. It was this which limited its performance on road and road circuits, although quarter-mile times were not too dusty; 15 seconds at around 95mph.

Even so, when *Car and Driver* ran a comparison test in early 1966 they found that the Skylark was slowest on track and strip when matched up to five other cars which were all within 12ci of each other around the 400-inch mark. The Skylark lost out to the Ford GTA, Olds 4-4-2, Chevelle SS396, the GTO and a Mercury Comet Cyclone at everything except braking, in which it outpointed all the competition. Although the bulk of the musclecar output – no matter which factory it came from – was continually criticized for poor braking capability, it was not a great selling point for Buick to be able to say that their car stopped better than the rest – stopped better than it went, almost.

And it must be remembered that the performance war between the big makers was by now just that – war. When *Car and Driver* ran their comparison test they booked three days of track and strip testing with eight cars from various makers, and issued their own written rules that the cars should be factory stock, or have modifications which could be purchased at any dealership. It was at this point that

Chrysler pulled out, and other makers began to bend the rules. Ford submitted a 'stock' GTA which had been prepared by Holman & Moody and Lincoln-Mercury had their Comet Cyclone prepared by NASCAR wizard Bud Moore. Probably both had spent as much – maybe even more – money preparing two 'showroom' cars for a press test as they would for a serious race, which is an indication of just how seriously the competition was fought. As *Car and Driver* observed, the two Fords were 'armed to the teeth.'

It was not much of a surprise to find that the Skylark fared badly against this kind of action, but all the cheating in the world wouldn't have made up for the basic Skylark faults in transmission and springs, nor concealed the fact that the big 401 was truthfully underpowered.

In 1967 there were two Buick introductions which would change the situation. One was the biggest Buick engine ever – the 430 V8, which was introduced as standard on the Wildcat and the Riviera, in which form it was no more powerful than previous engines, but supposedly ran more quietly and delivered its power more smoothly. There was also a cast-iron V8 of 400 inches displacement which was

Top: The 1969 GS 350 carried the engine, but the 1970 GSX (**above**) looked the part as well. The badgework was an important part of the musclecar creed.

built for the Special/Skylark series chassis and which appeared in the new Buick muscle contender. Called simply the GS400, it was available as either a convertible, a hardtop or a pillar coupe, and there was also a hardtop GS340 which, no surprise, ran the smaller 340 motor. Sales of this line were excellent (560,000 in the first model year) pushing Buick up to fifth place in the industry.

The GS400 developed 340hp, which left it relatively underpowered for its high (4175lbs) weight and it had a top speed of about 116mph, with quarter times falling around 15.5 seconds/90mph. The disk brakes were now generally held to be inadequate, probably as a result of the high all-up weight, and ride was poor, even on the freeway. The attempts to give the car a suspension and spring balance which would be capable of handling the weight resulted in a ride which was harsh for American tastes, and the power steering was frequently described as sloppy.

There were, unusually for a car of this character, no real options to correct or conceal any of the car's shortfalls. The 400ci iron block was only available on the GS400 and was the only powerplant supplied for it; there were no performance options to give it more beef. And though 4-speed manual was an option over standard 3-speed manual, the only auto option was the same sludgy old two-speed, and GM's 3-speed Turbo-Hydramatic was strangely unavailable.

There were changes for the next model year, when the 340 engine was dropped in favor of the slightly larger 350, which was now fitted with heads, intake manifold and exhaust manifolds taken from the big 430. This was a move primarily aimed at controlling exhaust emissions, but had the added benefit of producing a noticeable power bonus as well. Even so, as long as the 340hp 400-inch engine was underpowered for the car's weight, even the new 350 meant that the GS350 hardly qualified for the musclecar market.

And oddly enough the 350 handled better; something which was odd not because it may be expected with a lower overall weight and lighter front end, but because spring rates were higher than on the 400. But *Motor Trend*, in 1967, found the GS Buicks to be good on handling, second only to the GTO, they felt. This is hardly a typical reaction, especially since the GTO had more than its fair share of detractors where handling was concerned, but still, the magazine testers liked the overall handling characteristics, and ascribed to the heavy duty suspension the relatively new situation of cornering control by the driver rather than the car. At the same time they did point out that the feel of the car (and its contemporaries) was not totally different to the feel of the hotrods they'd been building using parts which were anything up to 25 years old. Quite correctly, they decided that it was all a question of approach, and were fully aware that all domestic car handling was the result of the Great American Compromise, in which Detroit tried to strike a balance between the fleet nimbleness of the imports and the soggy comfort to which purchasers of the full-size domestics were by now addicted.

And still on such a heavy car the standard brakes were finned drums all round; the power front disk/rear drum system which outperformed the stock setup with ease was

By the early seventies the thing was almost over. There's little difference between the 71 GS (**top**) and the 72 (**below**).

still nothing more than an option. And the GS cars looked heavy, too. The styling, while an attempt at the flowing lines of the traditional Ponycar fastback, was little better than cumbersome, although this didn't seem to detract from sales; indeed, 1969, which saw no major change to the GS cars, was a record year for Buick, in which they sold more cars than any other year of the sixties.

Throughout the era the Buicks made their play for the musclecar market and succeeded only in part. Although they were frequently called up for comparison tests in the press they almost always fared badly. Taken alone the cars seemed to impress with their combination of power, ride and handling, but always failed to meet the basic requirement of brute power when matched against the genuine full-blooded material. In part this may be due to the Buick corporate attitude, which did not deeply involve itself with racing, since its major markets were perceived to be above that level. Consequently when test cars were called for, Buick sent stock items. Other manufacturers, as we have seen, did not always do this, and probably sent hot factory cars even when no comparison was involved.

Even so Buick did not have a vast selection of performance parts available over the counter, did not have a huge dealer backup program to support private racers of their products, and did not not depend on pure muscle to sell them in the first place.

In fact, of all the musclecar builders, Buick were possibly the least perturbed by the gas shortages, the incursion of emission control laws and the general demise of the muscle market.

PONTIAC

GM were not too quick off the mark when it came to meeting the Mustang threat. The supremacy of Corvette, which was alone in the domestic two-seat market and had already beaten off a lone attack from the T-Bird years before, must have given them the secure feeling that whatever happened, T-Bird's successor could do them no harm. The far-sighted Bunkie Knudsen, by now Chevrolet general manager, was pushing for a car to rival Mustang, and eventually GM allowed Chevrolet the F-car, but the delay meant that Mustang would go unchallenged for years.

In fact when Mustang came out the initial industry reaction around Detroit was more than dubious; nobody could see any real merit in size or shape of the car and nobody expected it to do much at all. But they were wrong, and within weeks everybody in America, from teenagers to little old ladies (from Pasadena or elsewhere) was driving a Mustang. Demand outstripped supply by fifteen to one!

It was that which triggered the Chevrolet reply, the F-car which was to become Camaro by the time it hit the street.

Pontiac had their own ideas about a sportscar, however, and had a stronger performance background than most on which to base it. The Tempest, launched in 1961 and originally a compact, though like other small cars grew into an intermediate. It became *Motor Trend*'s Car of the Year straight away thanks to its revolutionary transaxle, fed by an equally revolutionary flexible torsion-tube driveshaft. *Motor Trend* also felt that its other Detroit first (well, post-war first, anyway), a four-cylinder engine, was another trend-setter which everyone in Motor City would be copying, and in this they couldn't have been more wrong, at least during the next two decades. And although the first Tempests sold well, the later models, up to intermediate size and equipped with a straight six, sold even better.

But it was the hot Tempests, with increasingly larger V8 engines, which led through the LeMans to the GTO and started the musclecar boom, moving in completely the opposite direction to the reasoning behind the *MotorTrend* award. With this sort of innovative performance background Pontiac were widely expected to come up with something really special as their response to the Mustang, and Pontiac themselves were determined to do so. Under the leadership of John DeLorean, Pontiac was a bustling concern; things were beginning to roll, and one of those things was a theory which became a brief but which was by no means original. One of the oldest Detroit lodestones was the desire to produce a neat and nimble two seat sportscar which could take on the imports at performance and handling and duck below them on price. It was the age-old dream to catch the kids while they were still on campus with a car which would appeal to their instincts and be easily within reach of their pockets. Catch them young, hook them on the marque, and keep them for life.

It was Bunkie Knudsen who had seen the youth market

coming, and now it was DeLorean pitching to the GM top brass, pointing out that the postwar baby boom was about to become a teenager boom, and that during the sixties there would be a record number of 16-year-olds in America. In 1964 400,000 new cars were bought by people under 25; almost 20 percent of licensed drivers in the USA were under 25. Both these percentages were increasing rapidly. It was the same ethos which had fired the Corvette builders, the same one which had sent Ford chasing after them once and the same reasoning behind Lee Iacocca's successor to the two-seat T-Bird.

Pontiac had been looking towards this market for a while, and had even produced their own prototype two-seater which was loosely based around some Corvette components but used simpler construction methods for its fiberglass bodyshell. Designated XP-833 it was, with only minor changes to lighting and grille, the shape which would be the '68 facelift for Corvette. But at the time it was made it was, in the finest traditions of GM, kept secret, even when two cars, SP-3 and SP-4 were built with fiberglass shells made by Dow-Smith at Ionia, Michigan. It was to this car that Pontiac turned to meet the Mustang head-on, and they wanted no part of the corporate badge-engineering policy which was pushing them towards a slightly reworked version of the Chevrolet F-Car. The proposal which DeLorean made to GM hierarchy gave this car a

Above: Pontiac followed Chevrolet's Camaro into the Ponycar market with their Firebird lookalike, despite DeLorean's opposition.

base price of $2500 using 80 percent Tempest parts, estimated production around 32,000 units in the first year and said that the car was already far enough advanced to be ready for the 1967 model year.

When that was turned down Pontiac proposed a four-seat version of the same car, decidedly upmarket, but still goodlooking. Even as this proposal was being made Pontiac design engineers were working on the F-Car, just in case . . . DeLorean's next gambit, a Pontiac version of the

Corvette, was also being worked on by Pontiac design, also in secret. Quite why Pontiac were willing to do a cosmetic job on Corvette but not Camaro is not clear, but after one last stand-up row with GM vice president Ed Cole the final decision was made, and Pontiac's competitor in the Pony-car league would be a Camaro-based four-place which was nowhere near as good-looking as Pontiac's home-grown material.

To begin with, Camaro itself was so late that although due for '67 launch it was already possible to base it almost entirely on the '68 Nova. It was this which left it tall around the A-Pillar and short along the hood, handicapping it from the start with dimensions which were completely at odds with the Ponycar style established by Ford. Although Chevrolet were pleased with the skin they had thrown over Nova's bones (and, when it made its debut, so were most of the people who saw it) Pontiac didn't like it. They gave it bigger wheels and tires, and lowered the suspension, a move which not only improved looks but also handling.

And handling did need some help; the single-leaf rear spring standard on Camaro was cheap to make but had no tuning flexibility – it could not be stiffened or softened to help overall ride or all-out performance handling – and left

Below: In 1970 Firebird too got a facelift which kept its appearance in line with Camaro.

The 1969 Firebird 400 convertible, with quad lamps and Endura front, showing heavy touches of the legendary Goat.

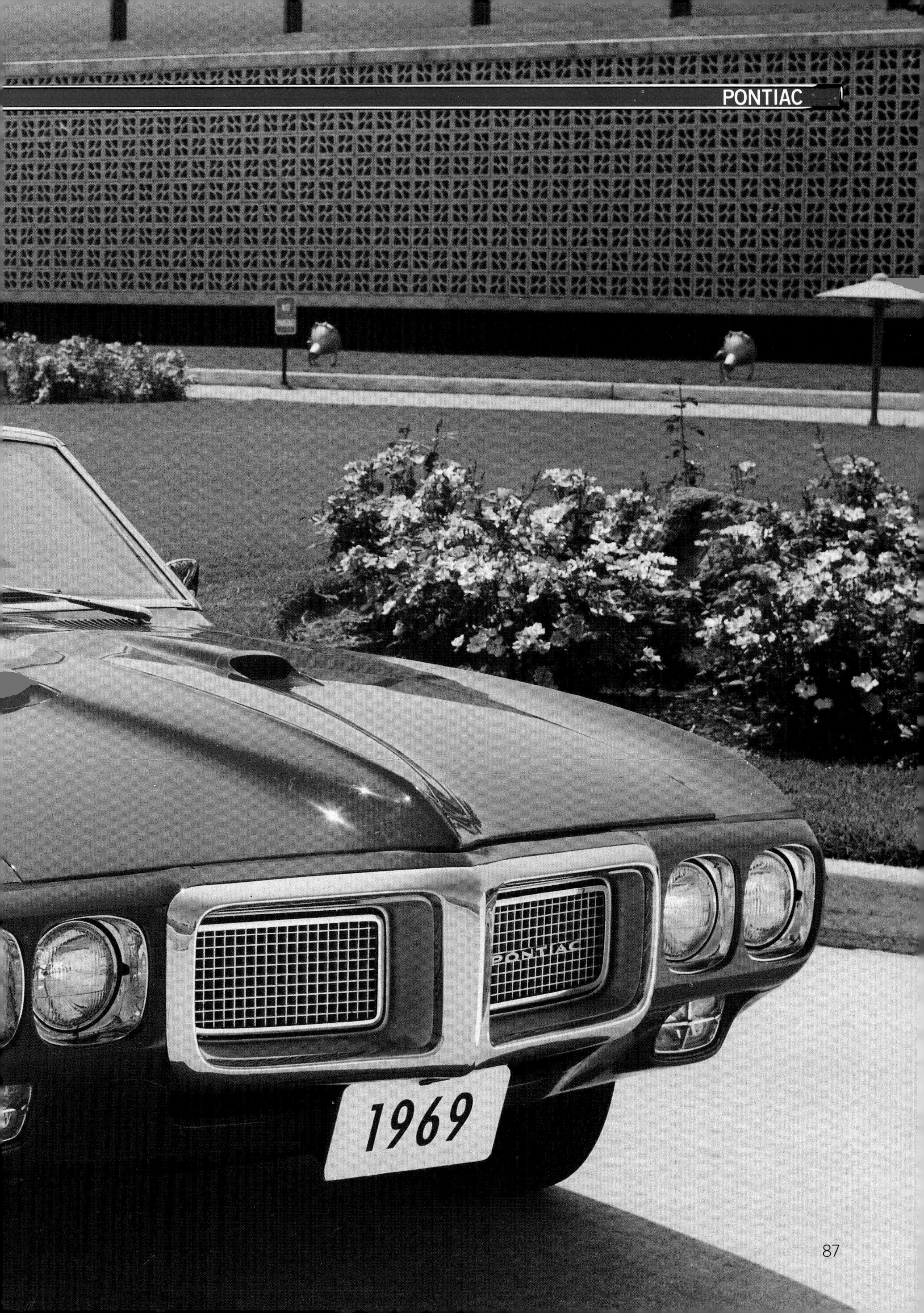
PONTIAC
1969

the car susceptible to wheel hop under acceleration and braking. Pontiac's solution was traction bars (fitted to '67 models as options) and multi-leaf rear spring with staggered shocks, which were not ready in time for the '67 launch of the car.

In fact the car missed the launch of the '67 lineup (which took place in September 1966) entirely, and in mid-October was made available to selected journalists at the GM proving grounds. Then in December Pontiac made the official announcement that Firebird would be available in five versions for 1967. Slightly more expensive than the Mustang and the Barracuda, Firebird was also more expensive than the Camaro; even with one of the optional V8 engines it was still cheaper than the Mercury Cougar or the V8 Marlin, which made it the top-of-the-range Ponycar. Addition of the optional 400ci V8 pushed it through into the luxury price bracket.

But at this stage the engine was not the big 360-horse monster optional to GTO buyers, but a comparatively milder 335hp item standard to the Firebird 400 and the Bonneville. And there was a reason for that. Quite simply, GM policy said that none of their products could have more than one hp per ten lbs of vehicle weight, so the engine had to be restricted as it was fitted to Firebird but not in the heavier GTO. This was achieved by fitting a soft metal tab on the Quadrajet carb which anybody in the know could break off with their fingers and find another 25hp.

However mild it might have seemed in standard, restricted, form, the engine managed to push the Firebird up to respectable quarter times, despite the fact that this late in the musclecar era the smog controls and regulations were already having demonstrably adverse affects on the performance of all auto engines.

By 1968 there was a Firebird 400 HO (High Output) with semi-elliptic rear springs and adjustable Konis to help handling and – at last – a three-speed console-mounted automatic box to replace the column-mounted two-speed which was common to most of GM's sporty range and which had made even high-power engines turn in appallingly slow times in cars not fitted with the Hurst manual option.

Car and Driver still found that back end stability was inconsiderate when they tested the car in early 1968, but that didn't stop them booting the car to 14-second quarters at just over 100mph, nor finding that it was the best-handling car out of a comparison test of six, which included an SS396 Camaro. In fact the Firebird was the only car to score top marks for cornering ability in the *Car and Driver* checklist. But in the same breath as they said that the Firebird was the car they'd all liked best out of the six – 'for sheer enjoyment and confidence behind the wheel the Firebird was almost in a class by itself' – they also pointed out that it was the second most expensive (behind Camaro). They also mentioned – not for the first (or last) time – that preparation on the Firebird was 'absolutely out of sight.' 'Preparation' in this case included, among other things, a number of adjustments to the engine timing which certainly helped it along but which also meant that it was outside the smog laws and not even street legal. And you can bet there were no metal tabs on the carburetor.

But it still was a fine performer, especially if the press features of the time are to be believed, although there is a strong temptation to think that there were perhaps very few press test vehicles which were actually delivered to the magazines in anything like stock showroom condition. How else could a tester suggest that a 330-horse 400 with Ram Air could take on a 425hp Mopar hemi car which weighed virtually the same as the Firebird? Unless what he had just been testing was not a stock 330hp Firebird.

In fact Royal Pontiac, from Royal Oak, Michigan, produced a $200 package which they called Royal Bobcat, and with that fitted *Car and Driver*'s Brock Yates concluded that the car was 'in the same league' as the big-inch Corvettes and the Mopar hemis.

Whatever the truth the Firebird sold exceptionally well, and number 50,000 rolled off the Lordstown, Ohio, line ten weeks after the car's launch, and the model year saw production reach more than 80,000, topping to 113,000 after a full 12 months although the figures were only good until compared with Camaro's 200,000-plus sales. To be fair, though, the GM cake had been divided 60-30 in favor of Chevrolet long before the cars had gone on sale.

The next year saw Pontiac leaning towards race involvement, although by now the GM no-racing directive had been strengthened to include instant dismissal for anyone caught at it, and promised links with Brabham failed to come out of the closet as a result. The 400 HO engine became a Ram Air HO 11, which developed 366hp in the GTO but only 340 in Firebird. Once again there was a 25hp instant boost available to anyone who could find the metal tab . . . 1969 was the first facelift year for what was still a comparatively young car, and saw Firebird put on two inches in length and grow to a 60-inch rear track. It was also the advent of the one-piece plastic front, although the GM Endura soft noses, which featured on Corvette, were too expensive and the designers settled for Lexan, which

Above left: The Trans Am was originally just an option package, Pontiac's answer to the Z28 Camaro.
Below: By the early 70's there was the Firebird 400 HO; the Trans Am had become a marque in its own right.

was cheaper, and rock-hard. There was a new version of the 400 Ram Air, but it wasn't Ram Air III – it was Ram Air IV, because in pre-production it was going to have four cold air inlets, although only two made it to the line. But the name stuck. It had four-bolt mains, forged aluminum pistons, heavy duty rockers, aluminum intake manifold and a fairly wild cam. Once again it was rated at only 345hp, but everyone who knew . . . It was also decidedly big-league power, partly grown out of last year's secretive and abortive attempts to go racing, and by any definition a heavyweight member of the muscle brigade. But it was by no means the ultimate development of the Firebird, although that would not be long in coming. And when it came, it would grow into a make all by itself . . . Trans Am.

But 1971 was another year. The shape remained more or less unchanged, although there were one or two extra vents here and there. And hot news should have been that last year's 345hp Trans Am engine was no longer the big

The 1972 Firebird Formula.

option; now there was a massive 455, conservatively rated the previous year at 370hp for the Catalina, Bonneville and Grand Prix. In 1971, though, and as fitted to the Trans Am, it was quoted at a low 335hp. And outputs of all the other engines were down. And as a clear concession to the insurance companies, who were highly interested in horsepower/weight relationships, the sales literature and advertising material also began to show two different hp ratings — one gross and one net. The gross figure was the one which Detroit had previously always quoted and sold on and was obtained on a dyno from a blueprinted engine stripped of engine-driven ancilliaries. The net figure included things like generator, water pump, and cooling fan. It could make as much as 100hp difference to the rated output of an engine once it was installed in a car. On the Firebird lineup it meant that the 350ci 2bbl was rated at 250hp gross but only 180hp net. The 455 was 325hp gross or 255 net. There was no difference in output involved, but the net figures, quoted to insurance companies, sounded a whole lot safer (and cheaper) than the gross figures.

Whichever way it was quoted, last year's 400ci engine was down by approximately 45-50hp, depending on which version it was. And there was a reason for that. Compression ratios were down from nearly 11:1 to 8:1. With no knife in sight the musclecars were emasculated with surgical precision.

Although ponycar sales, the midway bracket between family compacts and full-house musclecars, had been experiencing a constant fall in sales due to a gradual downward slide in demand, the same was not true of the musclecars, the real high-performers. Demand for these cars was as high now as it had ever been. Despite the onslaught of frightening insurance rates (prompted by equally frightening accident rates), the increased cost of purchase and the generally growing disapproval of the cars, the young buyers still wanted them and were still prepared to pay for them. And as long as that was true, Detroit would go on making them.

But the Government knew best and was prepared to force people who didn't agree to simply do what they were told. And if people couldn't be persuaded not to buy the cars then they would have to be made to. Federal control had arrived in a big way.

1972 was even worse. Horsepower (from now on only quoted as a net figure) advertising was gone, and Firebird practically vanished as well. Overall Pontiac slipped from third place in the sales league and stayed down. A major strike at Lordstown chopped Firebird and Camaro production and meant that more than 1000 cars waiting on the line had to be scrapped because they were too late to be '72 models and were illegal under '73 regulations. In 1970 the Firebird sales literature had vanished, and was incorporated into the general Pontiac performance catalog, but in 1971 there was no performance catalog for it to be in. The musclecar was finished.

The absence of the 303 tunnel port seriously affected the racing program. Naturally this was nothing to do with Pontiac, and was all done by Titus/Godsall racing. Even so Pontiac tried to get the SCCA to accept the 25-odd engines which had been specially made as homologated items for

the '69 season and — unsurprisingly — failed. The team raced with the Chevrolet motor installed, and couldn't even run the '69 body style since SCCA rules called for 1000 to have been built and that hadn't happened either. However you look at it, this was not a good season for the Trans Am, although the race car came in third at the Daytona 24-hour behind two experimental Lola race cars, which was no small achievement but did not count as part of the SCCA Trans Am season. During that season the Firebirds didn't manage to win a single race between them although they placed 3rd in the manufacturers' championship with 32 points. Second-placed Ford had 64 points and Chevrolet, heavily disguised behind the Penske outfit, won with 78.

By 1970, as the facelift model was due out, Pontiac knew that there was no hope that they could get away from a corporate car at this stage, having failed to fend off the F-car in the beginning, so once again their hopes of producing anything completely individual were, at best, slim. What they could, and did, do was insist on full cooperation during design, to give themselves an overall voice in the shaping of the new car and also make it possible to ensure that the new Firebirds would be as different from the cheaper Camaro as possible.

Chevrolet had started work on the follow-up to Camaro in 1966 — before the first-generation model was out on the street. Pontiac started almost a year later and produced a clay which was so appealing that it became the base around which the second-generation F-Car from both divisions was based. Due out in 1970, it was late, and missed its fall launch, finally appearing in March the next year and becoming the 70-1/2 model.

Its base engine was the Chevrolet straight six, there was also a 265hp 350 V8 and there were no less than four different versions of the 400ci motor available. There was a stock 2bbl version rated at a miserable 265hp and obviously hiding something, a 4bbl version which delivered 330hp, which was more realistic and represented quite a jump, a 335hp Ram Air version and finally a 345hp engine which was standard to the Trans Am.

Its handling package included thick sway bars front and rear as well as stiffer shock absorbers and rear springs, and the Trans Am was now one of only four Firebird options; the others were the stock Firebird, the Firebird Esprit and the Firebird Formula 400.

The Trans Am was still the fully-loaded option and its purpose in life was to be an image-maker for the lower-priced options, to bring people into dealer showrooms and also to get the racing parts necessary to success in the SCCA series homologated. But there was a major drawback to this latter, and that was quite simply price. It was an expensive car and in '69 only 800 of the Trans Am Firebirds had been sold. In 1970 it was necessary to sell 3200 of them to gain SCCA approval, and F James McDonald, who had replaced John DeLorean when he was moved up into Chevrolet, decided that it could be done and instructed the sales force to do it; they did.

Right: 1974 was the year that Firebird and Trans Am (and Camaro, come to that) got the steeply raked and pointed plastic fronts which would carry the styling until the massive 1981 redesign. This is the Firebird 400.

Then Chevrolet stole their spoilers after DeLorean did a deal with McDonald, and tricked the SCCA into allowing them for racing even though they had, at the time, produced not one single car with the rear deck spoiler like the one on their race Z-28. But despite the enthusiastic reception which the new car received from the press (*Car and Driver* were particularly enthusiastic, especially about the handling), even though the stock Trans Am with a four-speed manual covered the standing quarter 14/103mph, the race season was so bad for the Trans Am that it's better forgotten.

By the end of the sixties the pin pressed up against the musclecar bubble by the Naderites and others was on the point of puncturing its fabric and bursting it permanently. Insurance company reaction to the massive horsepower of the big-inch musclecar V8 engines had already produced a situation in which the car makers had, without telling outright lies, presented their engine outputs in the most favorable light.

There were even situations in which various divisions within large combines were employing more than one or two dubious tricks to get around their own corporate policies, which were by now firmly against racing and also against high-horsepower power plants in small cars. Emission controls were proliferating; air injection pumps were everywhere, the sealed emission carburetor was making its debut, low-compression engines were taking over from high, and engine timing was being altered to suit low-octane gas and produce lower emissions at the expense of power.

So when Pontiac announced – very quietly indeed, with the lowest of low profiles, the advent of the Firebird Trans Am, it was little more than a cosmetic package of striping for the Firebird 400. There was no hint, not even to GM, that this was meant to replace the two-seat all-out sports-car which Pontiac had been trying to make when the Camaro F-Car was forced on them from above. Not even the fact that it was evocatively named after the famous SCCA series in which Chevrolet's thinly-disguised Z-28 racer had enjoyed so much success alerted anyone to the true nature of the beast which now confronted them.

Above: The Trans Am's new look for 1974 had hardly altered by 1979 (**below**). The real changes were under the hood, where the stringent legislation had emasculated its low-compression engine.

The fact is that the 400-inch engine was well outside the Trans Am series 5-liter capacity limit made it an odd choice of name, but the truth was that a 303 tunnel-port engine under development just never made it into production; the T/A was simply too late. But it was intended to happen, and it would then have been Pontiac's contender in the series, and doubtless every bit as quick as the Z-28 Camaro, possibly more so.

Basic reasoning for Trans Am was closely allied to the thinking which had seen the launch of the high-stepping GTO sales booster, a cosmetic package called The Judge, launched to help flagging sales of the Goat at a time when sales of musclecars generally were beginning to take a nosedive.

In true muscle tradition a Trans Am was not a car; it was an option package, but after the first year it was more than just stripes. On top of the base car you had to order the Ram Air engine plus front disks which were mandatory with that option, variable ratio power steering which allowed easy parking but still kept the driver in touch with the road at speed, and a limited-slip rearend. The dress-up kit for the outside — which signaled to the world that this was no ordinary Firebird — included as one option the Trans Am hood, front air dam, rear wing, air extractors for the fenders, stiffer springs and shocks, fiberglass-belted tires, sport steering wheel, and those emblems and stripes.

Apart from an information insert for existing dealer literature there was no printed information on Trans Am available, and first year sales reflected its more or less secret debut completely accurately and only 697 — including the only eight Trans Am convertibles ever made — came off the line. In 1970 the situation was slightly improved, although Trans Am remained a Firebird option. Along with the slightly milder Formula 400, the Trans Am was the performance route for Firebird buyers which got them a 345hp 400 V8 in a striped-up body with air dams and a shaker hood generally looking rather impressive.

It impressed the press and other testers, who found that it was probably the first domestic car to have taken on the ride/handling compromise and beaten it fair and square. Unlike most of the musclecars and ponycars with the tough handling packages it was not harsh to ride in, nor bouncy and boomy. Yet the suspension really did do the right stuff when the going got serious, even to the point that *Hot Rod* said they thought the handling was now beyond the psychological limits of most of the people who would drive it — something *Hot Rod* thought would go some way to preventing the kind of horrific accidents which had haunted the musclecar all its life and done much to earn the breed in general the disapproval of everyone in America apart from enthusiasts and people with their own wrecking business.

DODGE

By the end of the musclecar era Dodge had established themselves as one of the leading names in the US high-performance market. As the De Soto had faded through the fifties and finally died in '61, the Dodge division had pushed upwards into the sector for its upmarket products and had also been quick to spot and exploit the performance market. While the Lancer version of the Chrysler Valiant was introduced in 1961 as their compact they had offered the intermediate size Dart the year before on a 118-inch wheelbase, running a slant six as standard with a 318 V8 as an option. The company had introduced a 241 V8 in 1953 and had evolved a variety of assorted displacements from it until there were a 361 and a (very) high-output 383 (which racked up an astonishing 330hp) as well as the Chrysler 361 available for the full-size cars in 1960.

Two four-barrel carburetors and a cold air induction system were largely responsible for the big output of the 383 engine and it already made the full-size Polara a very quick car, with a top speed of 120mph. Oversize Chrysler brakes made it a safe top speed and torsion bar suspen-

sion at the front end conspired to make Polara a handy car to drive. Naturally the ram-air engine was made available as an option on the Dart by 1961, which made it an extremely rapid piece of work. The Dart stayed a top-line performer and years later would be regarded by many as the neatest of what Dodge were by then calling their 'Scat Pack,' as well as being one of their quickest cars. It was even then still doing well with a smallish engine, at 340ci, and turned in the sort of performance which would be natural to the big-inch musclecars, even though 340 in-

Above: The 1967 Charger, into the ponycar market alongside Mustang.
Right: The 67 Dart hardtop and the convertible (**below**) had the slab-sided look of a car in need of a facelift.

ches hardly qualified as muscle when lined up with the 426, 427, 428, 429, 440 and 454 monsters which were by then vying for top honors.

Some of this was due to Virgil Exner's economical design capability which trimmed 400lbs from the 1962 Dart facelift; and which resulted in a car which had lost six inches overall and was built on a chassis two inches shorter than before, at 116 inches. Exner was ahead of his time though (by about 20 years), and the range didn't do too well. It was resized again – upwards, this time – and was powered by some new, bigger engines which had been introduced the year before. There was a 413ci wedge for the full-size cars,

although not Dart, and likewise proscribed for the already zippy intermediate was the overbored 426 ramcharger hemi. With aluminum pistons and a high-lift cam it produced a highly respectable 425hp and secured endless titles for Dodge, including the 1962 NHRA championship. On every dragstrip across America the big motor was the supreme killer of the season. It was the outright wonder of NASCAR, where Dodge and Plymouth campaigned extensively, and secured a 1-2-3 victory at Daytona in 1964.

There was a minor facelift for Dart in '65, and the mid-range cars, now on a 117-inch wheelbase, were renamed Coronet. The hot news for the performance enthusiasts

was the no-holds-barred Coronet Hemi Charger. This came on its own special 115-inch chassis and was one of the best high-speed bargains in the entire musclecar story, with a base price of just over $3100 when it was introduced. It was a 2-door sedan and had heavy-duty springs and shock absorbers, a heavy sway bar, four-speed gearbox and super-strong brakes developed for Police chase cars. Like the Polara before it, top speed was 120mph and 0-60 time was around seven seconds, all of which was pulled from a 430hp version of the street hemi. Its arrival

heralded another year of racetrack domination for Dodge.

1966 saw little change; 318 was the stock option, but the other, larger engines were still available. '67 was a year of small facelift for the bulk of the Dodge range, leaning towards clean lines. The Charger stayed the same, and the normal Coronet also grew an R/T version which had heavy duty suspension and wider tires as standard backup to the 440-inch, 375hp V8 which was standard. Both Coronet and Charger had the hemi option.

1968 external changes were major, resulting in a completely restyled Coronet and Charger which were among the best-looking Dodge cars of the entire decade. The Charger was a semi-fastback which did exceptionally well out of its single 4-barrel 440, giving a useful 375hp. The result was a top speed of about 120mph and 14/95mph quarters out of a 3-speed Chrysler Torqueflite automatic box. Good-looking as it was, it was a heavy car underneath – all 4400lbs of it, and even 6-leaf springs and stiff shocks, plus thick sway bars, couldn't conceal that from its driver. The wide tires went some way to giving it back some cornering stability, but there's no getting round the fact

Above left: The 1968 Dart GT still looked old-fashioned.
Top right and below: The 1968 Charger, complete with 426 street hemi, looked more like it.

1969 DART

Top left: The 'aerodynamic' Daytona Charger from 1969 looked as powerful as it was. The Dart (**bottom left**) still needed some new sheetmetal. The Super Bee (**above and left**) was another decal exercise which looked good.

that the Charger was tail-heavy, with an inconsistent and therefore unpredictable tendency to swap ends. Even with optional front disks and large rear drums, braking left quite a lot to be desired.

Power steering, which was largely optional at the time across all makes, was vital to the big-block cars, but where most of Detroit was busy chasing after the progressively decreasing power perfected in Europe, the Charger, which felt reassuringly in touch with the road at low speeds, simply got lighter and lighter, making it even harder for gung-ho drivers to decipher the intentions of the back end.

In the light of that, it's clear that the suspension compromise was in action once again, and the Charger's ride was thus excellent, but if the 440 left it unstable on a circuit, the hemi could be downright dangerous.

The Coronet R/T looked a bigger and heavier car, with seeming acres more sheetmetal, but the convertible (which was not a Charger option) weighed in at an outrageous 4200lbs – actually a few hundred lbs more than the Charger – and thus even with the same degree of beef in the handling package it still only performed adequately for a large car in turns. Combined with the big engines, the 'handling package' raised handling ability to a barely acceptable minimum. While straight-line performance was startlingly good (even though there was a vast amount of axle wind-up under hard acceleration) this was never a car for going circuit-racing in.

The Dart GTS was a different story. With the baby 340-inch engine replaced by the huge 375hp 440 it had a top end in excess of 120mph, did 100 in 15 seconds dead and managed quarters in low fourteens at just below 100mph. Although the 426 hemi gave an extra 55hp it also weighed in at an extra 150lbs or so, giving it a handling disadvantage and making it virtually a race-only option. *Car Life* tested the 440-engined GTS in early 1968 and found the handling 'as close to neutral as is practical in a car designed to be driven by people of minimal ability.' Predictability, unlike its bigger stablemate, was 'outstanding.' Low curb weight – 3300lbs – was clearly a significant factor here, as it clearly also meant that the same front disk/rear drum braking arrangements acted far better when attached to this than to the Charger or Coronet.

All the times which *Car Life* recorded were reached with

Above: The Challenger R/T convertible, plus 383 Magnum powerplant, proving that muscle could be elegant too.

the cars bearing standard Chrysler Torqueflite automatic transmission and, with one exception, stock rearend ratios. By using the option boxes on the order blank it was possible to get a wilder axle and a manual four-speed transmission which gave at least a five percent power advantage and was clearly the route for weekend drag racers and full-time streetracers to go for. And they did, in high enough numbers to gain themselves a whole pack of strip honors once again, although the bulk of sales went out with the auto box fitted.

Along with the introduction of the Dart GTS came advanced versions of the rest of the Scat Pack, as Dodge adopted its Bumble Bee rear deck striping for family identification, and even included one model designated as the Super Bee. This was almost the econo-racer end of the market, with the 335hp 383ohv engine, and (presumably

Below: The 69 Coronet R/T, complete with bumble-bee stripes and ferocious 440 six-pack.

**STRIPED
VENTED
AND READY TO FLY
MUSCLE UP THIS YEAR WITH THE "FOUR PERFORMERS."**

First, you'll hear the satisfying low rumble.
Then you'll see the bumblebee tail stripes.
That's when you'll know
that Coronet R/T
and the Coronet Super Bee have arrived.
If you respond
to the surge of power from your machine
and thrill
to the feel of meshing gears,
then Coronet R/T is your kind of car.
Coronet R/T comes as a two-door hardtop or convertible.
These are the features:
A 440-cubic-inch Magnum V8 engine
with dual exhausts.
Your choice of two transmissions—
a rugged, slick-shifting four-speed manual box
or a heavy-duty three-speed TorqueFlite automatic.
Special wide-rim wheels
with the wide-tread tires. Bucket seats up front.
And you can add more.
If you want muscle on a budget,
fly with the new Coronet Super Bee.
Choose either two-door coupe or hardtop.
Then take off.
Coronet Super Bee is supered up with standard items
like the 383 Magnum engine,
four-speed manual shift,
high-performance Red Line F70 x 14 wide-tread tires,
and bumblebee stripes.
And with Coronet Super Bee, the best built-in feature
is the low price.
Whatever your choice,
you'll fly in style
with any of the 1969 Coronet R/T or Super Bee models.

Coronet Super Bee hardtop

Coronet R/T hardtop

Above: The 1970 Dart Swinger still looks humble compared to the 70 Daytona (**below**).

in deference to this comparative lightweight) lower-rate springing all round, which naturally gave it a lot more body roll than the rest of the Scat Pack. Even so it handled well, and felt good to drive, soon becoming a favorite among magazine testers and featuring prominently (and highly) in numerous comparison tests.

1970 saw the advent of the new Dodge contender in the ponycar stakes – the all-new Challenger, which was lower and shorter than any other Dodge, having a small 110-inch wheelbase. It was also, with the only possible exception of the fastback Charger, the best-looking member of the Scat Pack yet, with two-door sedan styling which struck a balance between trim family car and an armed-to-the-teeth supercar, and in this respect was styled years ahead of its time. Once again with one possible exception – Corvette – it was the only musclecar which still looks good to modern eyes. And make no mistake about it, despite being sized below the norm for the musclecar bracket, as a compact, it was decidedly a member of the clan.

Initially it was just Challenger and Challenger R/T which were available with a slant six standard and a 318 V8 optional in Challenger, against 383 as standard in the R/T.

Above: More period advertising. Dodge needed plenty to shout about at the time.

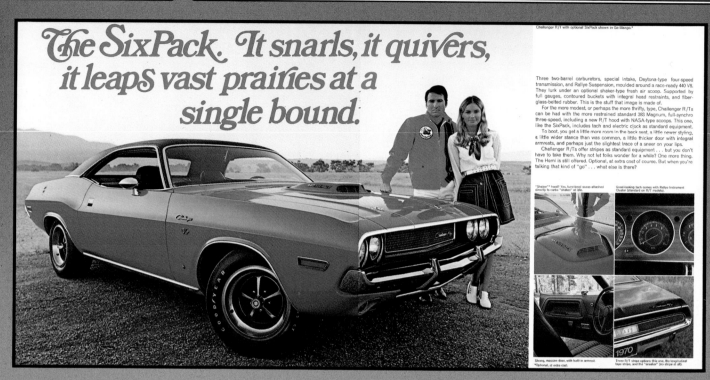

The SixPack. It snarls, it quivers, it leaps vast prairies at a single bound.

Challenger R/T with optional SixPack shown in Go-Mango.

Three two-barrel carburetors, special intake, Daytona-type four-speed transmission, and Rallye Suspension, moulded around a race-ready 440 V8. They lurk under an optional shaker-type fresh air scoop. Supported by full gauges, contoured buckets with integral head restraints, and fiber-glass-belted rubber. This is the stuff that image is made of.

For the more modest, or perhaps the more thrifty, type, Challenger R/Ts can be had with the more restrained standard 383 Magnum, full-synchro three-speed, including a new R/T hood with NASA-type scoops. This one, like the SixPack, includes tach and electric clock as standard equipment.

To boot, you get a little more room in the back seat, a little newer styling, a little wider stance than was common, a little thicker door with integral armrests, and perhaps just the slightest trace of a sneer on your lips.

Challenger R/Ts offer stripes as standard equipment . . . but you don't have to take them. Why not let folks wonder for a while? One more thing. The Hemi is still offered. Optional, at extra cost of course. But when you're talking that kind of "go" . . . what else is there?

"Shaker" hood? Yes, functional scoop attached directly to carbs "shakes" at idle.

Great-looking tach comes with Rallye Instrument Cluster (standard on R/T models).

*Strong, massive door, with built-in armrest. *Optional, at extra cost.*

Three R/T stripe options: this one, the longitudinal tape stripe, and the "sneaker" (no stripe at all).

1970

Above: The brochures still hinted at it, but they said nothing about performance or horsepower.

Enter Challenger '70.
The sports car with the big difference.

Above: The Challenger, with its 440 engine, delivered real muscle for those who were still interested.

Options for the R/T included everything which was available, right up to the 440 six-pack and on to the 426 hemi.

This compact was the hot number in the Dodge lineup, and was soon the subject of all kinds of special editions, and the first model year was witness to the Challenger Deputy and the Challenger T/A. This last was pointedly aimed at fans of the Trans Am series, although its over-limit 340 engine meant that it was only for those streetracers who wished to emulate their track heroes. Under the hood was a six-pack version of the V8 rated at 290hp with reinforced main bearing webs, specially modified heads and low-restriction exhausts. Power brakes, wide tires and Special Rallye suspension meant that it was an even keener performer than the ever-popular Dart, although the optional fast-ratio power steering was essential if the driver wanted to use the car properly.

Naturally it looked the part, bearing matt black fiberglass hood or a good looking shaker hood, rear deck lip spoiler and vast sidestripes bearing the '340 six-pack' emblem in huge oversized lettering. As Dodge themselves boasted in their advertising for the car it was indeed the 'end of the road for the do-it-yourself kit.' With its selection of engines so vast, powerful and respected, it's not surprising to find that the big-block options accounted for 40 percent of Challenger sales in the first year. This was in direct contradiction to most of the supercar league, and even the sports-committed Corvette sold mostly in its mid-range 'car-about-town' trim. No doubt at all, Challenger was getting straight through to its target and really grabbing the attention of the enthusiasts.

Apart from the arrival of a hardtop coupe, the Challenger went unchanged through '71 and it was only when the '72

models were announced that it became clear that Challenger was too late. The big engines were gone – in fact virtually all of the options were gone – and Challenger was offered with a choice of only three. The six was standard, and there were two V8s of either 318 or 340 cubic inches. And in this year the hp went down, thanks to the increased amount of smog gear on board, and was in any case now quoted net. The most powerful Challenger you could buy was no longer a 425hp firebreathing hemi but a lowly 240hp shopping trolley.

Above and below: The Challenger was one of the better-looking products of the musclecar phenomenon, but arrived too late to be a major contender. Like the massive Charger 500 (**right**) it has since found film immortality – Challenger in Vanishing Point, Charger in the less appealing Dukes of Hazzard.

THE END OF AN ERA

The musclecar phenomenon, which had kicked off with the arrival of Pontiac's Goat, lasted almost exactly ten years, and it's a surprise that it was able to sustain itself through even that long. Few of the cars were especially meritorious when considered overall, especially by modern standards but also by contemporary ones. It's surprising that so many people bought so many of them, and even more surprising, almost horrifying, that Detroit was prepared to go on making them.

But Detroit did just that, not only supplying an existing demand, but doing its best to fuel it, even create it where none had previously existed. Had it not been for the strenuous efforts directed into marketing it's entirely possible that there would have been no muscle boom at all. However it is equally unfair to dismiss the cars out of hand as simply a sales exercise; there were undeniably keen sports and car enthusiasts at work in the motor city and elsewhere whose dedication to the production of excellent cars was absolute. In all too few instances, however, their products made it onto the streets in the form which had been intended, and these are the truly great cars of the period. Out of these, the easiest example to spot is the one which stood head and shoulders above the rest of the pack at the time and is still an unequalled milestone in the history of the auto industry worldwide – Carroll Shelby's pure, racebred Cobra. For the bulk of them, though, the final production runs were allowed by corporate policy and financial necessity.

The fall in GTO sales, which began almost as soon as the car was launched, was partly due to the growing ecology lobby and to the increasing cost of insurance. The insurance companies had wised up quickly, and anything bearing the GTO emblems was hard or expensive to cover, as were an increasing number of other cars. And those competitors were the other reason for the fall in sales; to begin with there had been no competition at all, but once the GTO had set the pace no major manufacturer could afford to be left out and they all had a range of cars competing in the musclecar market. GM had several, and Pontiac's own Mustang-basher, the Firebird, was giving the GTO a hard time in the sales graphs. The Judge, a completely over-the-top cosmetic job, was designed to restore flagging sales, but it was almost too late.

If the Judge's stripes, spoiler and bright orange paint were aimed straight at the illegal streetracers on Connecting Avenue, Van Nuys and Woodward, the huge 455 engines was also pointing the same way. But already loaded with emission controls, redlined at 5100rpm and designed only for big-car luxury cruising, it was rated at only 360hp, less than some of the 400-inch options, and already a bell

was tolling. The following year saw the GM commitment to low-compression engines suitable for unleaded gas in line with the 1970 Clean Air Act. Sealed carburetors and evaporative emission control followed, and suddenly the performance car was dead. The Judge was discontinued, the GTO plastic front end was offered as an option on the LeMans. Soon Pontiac was hard at work shedding the GTO image which they had carefully built up and nurtured through the years. They weren't alone in this, as Chevrolet dumped the SS from Chevelle and Dodge scrapped the R/T designation. Then in late 1970 Ford abandoned most of its Trans-Am, USAC and NASCAR events, and began to tone down the Mustang to face the austerity to come, producing tame and weakened cars, allocating to the original Ponycar the same fate of emasculation suffered by its predecessor, the Thunderbird.

1970 saw what was likely to be musclecar's last fling, when Plymouth unveiled their final entry into the Rapid Transit System. Designed for the 200mph NASCAR speedways, the Superbird was the ultimate Road Runner. Dual quads atop the 426 hemi gave 425hp, and the 'bird had an aerodynamically-shaped droop-snoot concealing pop-up headlamps and a huge rear wing. Offered for one year only, a mere 1920 of them were built.

The 'bird was a follow-up to the '69 entry from the Dodge workshops. Again built for only one year, the Daytona Charger was built especially for the Daytona meeting, and it was this which lay behind the pointed nosecone and rear stabilizer. The Daytona Charger was around 20 percent more aerodynamically clean than the previous year's Charger which worked out that it was 500 yards better off each lap – an advantage well worth having. 505 of these cars were built – just the right number to homologate as a NASCAR production car, and running with its Plymouth cousin the Daytona and Superbird dominated the 1970 NASCAR season, winning 38 out of 48 races.

But it was a last, desperate fling. New Federal laws meant that the distinctive plastic fronts had to go, since steel bumpers would be required from '73 onwards, and the cars, like GTO, took yet another step backwards. Those which retained their plastic nosecones paid vast out-front weight penalties, forced to mount huge iron girders inside the plastic, robbing them of any function beyond pure cosmetics and adding more weight to the reinforcing beams carried in the doors. Soon even the mighty Goat was little more than an option in the LeMans range, and not much of an option at that. In 1973 Pontiac sold fewer GTOs than that original 5000 compromise allowed for in its first year, and 7000 in 1974. The oil embargo in 1973, which had pushed the pump price of gas up by 100 percent literally overnight, quite simply meant the end for the musclecars; the 74 GTO, with its baby 350 V8, still returned an unbelievably greedy 10mpg. In 1974, ten years after it had first appeared and set the street alight, the Pontiac GTO was terminated.

Historians and sociologists are all agreed that there was something very special about the sixties; it was a time of growth and of radical change, and it encompassed the explosion of the youth culture, marked the new young affluent society as the one which would set trends and determine tastes. But once the explosion was over and the dust was settled, there were no more points to make, no more arguments to win.

The early months of 1969 saw the gathering of half a million people in upstate New York for the biggest peace, love and music festival ever; Woodstock was, and is, important. But by December both the summer and the sixties were over, as the big gathering of the bands at Altamont, headed by the Rolling Stones, erupted into violence and death. By 1973, as the oil embargo struck and Americans began to shoot each other in the quest for gas, it was finished. Liddy and McCord had bungled the Watergate break-in, Henry Kissinger received his Nobel Peace Prize only days after the Yom Kippur war exploded across the middle east, and Arab terrorists killed more than 30 people in a machine-gun attack at Rome airport. The seventies were shaping up to be a whole lot nastier than the sixties.

The music industry's fever of excitement had given way to the tinsel of bubblegum music, perpetuated by a wave of no-hope, no-talent bands trying to follow the wave of exploitable nonsense launched by the likes of David Cassidy, the Osmonds, Slade, the Bay City Rollers, and David Essex.

And at the cinema one of the big box-office success stories was a film heavily based on the California cruising cult of the early sixties and totally dedicated to the street-racer's art and creed; with the last rumble of open headers only recently vanished from the street corner, *American Graffiti* was selling the nostalgia of an era hardly cold in its grave.

Goodbye to all that. The musclecar age lives on only for a few enthusiasts, who keep the cars on the road.

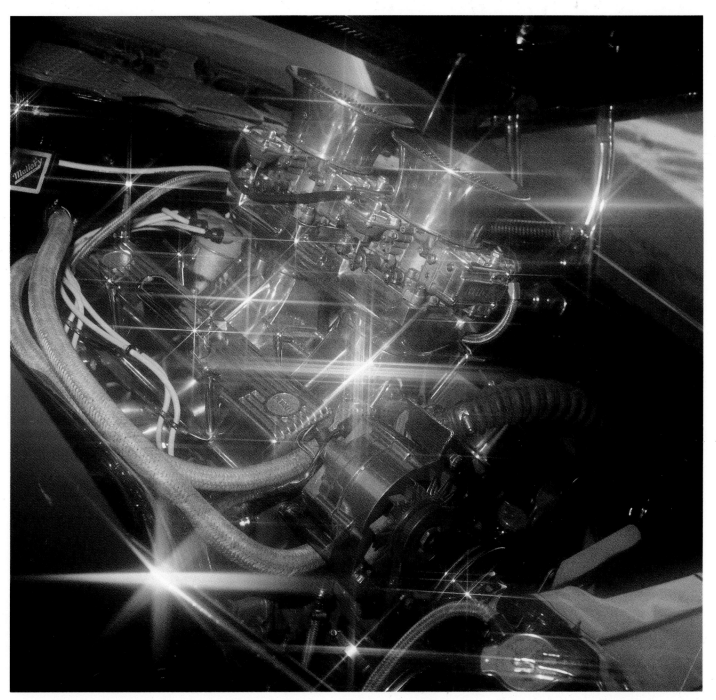

INDEX

Picture Credits